CW00733084

Fragrant Orchids

Fragrant Orchids

A Guide to
Selecting, Growing,
and Enjoying

Steven A. Frowine

TIMBER PRESS

Published in 2005 by
Timber Press, Inc.
The Haseltine Building
133 S.W. Second Avenue, Suite 450
Portland, Oregon 97204-3527, U.S.A.
www.timberpress.com
For contact information for editorial, marketing, sales, and distribution
in the United Kingdom, see www.timberpress.com/uk.

Printed in Hong Kong

Library of Congress Cataloging-in-Publication Data

Frowine, Steven A.
    Fragrant orchids : a guide to selecting, growing, and enjoying / Steven A. Frowine.
        p. cm.
    Includes bibliographical references (p.   ) and index.
    ISBN 0-88192-739-2 (hardback)
    1. Orchids. 2. Aromatic plants. 3. Orchid culture. I. Title.
    SB406.F67 2005
    635.9'344—dc22
                                                                2005001444

A catalog record for this book is also available from the British Library.

Contents

To my mother, Janet Allen Frowine, and deceased father,
Samuel E. Frowine, for encouraging me to pursue my love and
passion for the cultivation and appreciation of plants.
My father bought me my first orchids from
Alberts and Merkel Brothers in Boynton Beach, Florida,
when I was a teenager while on a family vacation.
He had a fluorescent light fixture installed in our basement
where I grew these orchids and other tropicals.
I truly felt my little "indoor greenhouse" was
a magical place.

And to my loving wife, Sascha, who shares my curiosity,
appreciation, and fascination with the natural world.
She has been my partner, staunch supporter,
and soul mate in discovering nature's wonders.

And to Janet and Paul Bowman, who gave me
my first job working in their greenhouses
in my hometown of Portsmouth, Ohio.
They were a generous, kind couple
who provided me a wonderful experience,
which sealed my decision that a life centered
on horticulture was my destiny.

Acknowledgments

The orchid community is a disparate group of people bound together by their common love of this extraordinary family of plants. Certainly, the history of orchid discovery as well as today's rapidly increasing interest in this group of plants proves that orchids have had and continue to have a very strong lure to anyone who sees them. Fortunately, unlike earlier days when orchids were expensive and information about them was a guarded secret, accessible only to a select few aristocrats, orchids have rapidly become plants that everyone can now enjoy and afford.

Most growers, amateur or professional, are free with their thoughts and opinions and are eager to have others join the orchid fraternity. For this I am very grateful for without this openness from the many amateur and professional orchid growers, this book would not have been possible. To the many people who have "lent their noses" and given their personal descriptions of scents that I received at the various orchids shows and gleaned through the literature, thanks!

I would like to recognize a few of the people who gave exceptional help:

My wife, Sascha, who read over and made suggestions of countless drafts and who put up with my driving obsession to bring this book to print.

Judy Becker, who, in reviewing my drafts, generously contributed her encyclopedic knowledge and eye for nomenclatural detail. She was of great help with this book.

Rita Buchanan, an amazing multi-talented Renaissance person, for her encouragement and horticultural and editing judgment.

Russ Vernon, a classmate of mine in the horticulture program at Ohio State University, who reviewed various proofs and lent his life-long orchid growing expertise.

Chapter 1

Fragrance Facts and Fancy

In the quiet valley I can see no orchids growing—
By accident, a gentle breeze betrays their presence.
It is a liberating fragrance, pure unsullied—
One sniff of it is enough to give enlightenment.

SuShih, eleventh-century Chinese poet,
"The Lonely Orchid"

The Sense of Smell Plays an Important Role in Our Lives

The Sense of Smell Institute states in its brochure, *Living Well with Your Sense of Smell* (1996), "Compared to our other senses, relatively little was known about our sense of smell and it was certainly the one most taken for granted."

Writers can sometimes express phenomena more comprehensibly to the lay person than can a scientist. Helen Keller wrote, "Smell is a potent wizard that transports us across thousands of miles and all the years that we have lived" (Sense of Smell Institute 1996).

A poet, Diane Ackerman, wrote in her book, *A Natural History of the Senses* (1990),

> Breaths come in pairs, except at two times in our lives—the beginning and at the end. At birth we inhale for the first time, at death we exhale for the last. In between, through all the lather of one's life, each breath passes air over our olfactory sites. Each day we breathe about 23,040 times and move around 438 cubic feet of air. It takes us about five seconds to breathe—two seconds to inhale and three seconds to exhale—

and in that time, molecules of odor flood through our systems. Inhaling and exhaling, we smell odors. Smells coat us, swirl around us, enter our bodies, emanate from us. We live in a constant wash of them.

Our sense of smell is most acute between the ages of 20 to 40. In general, men seem to have less perceptive noses than females. Three scientists from the Monell Chemical Senses Center in Philadelphia postulated that odor pleasantness evaluations were better perceived by the right nostril and that odor name or recognitions was perceived by the left nostril (Herz et al. 1999).

What Is Scent and How Is It Perceived?

The world is full of an impressive array of scents. The literature states that there are between 4,000 and 10,000 distinct odors, all of which humans can detect and are sensitive to.

Smell is said to be one of the "chemical senses" (the other being taste), since it depends upon chemicals to be triggered. Both of these senses are closely related; in fact, some scientists say that about 75 percent of taste is really smell. This is probably one of the reasons that many of the words we use to describe fragrances are actually favorite foods, such as coconut, chocolate, vanilla, oranges, candy, apples, bread, flavored soda, and chewing gum, or spices for foods, such as cinnamon.

Roy Genders, a venerable British horticulturist and writer, stated in his book, *Scented Flora of the World* (1977), in reference to plants,

> Scent is the oxidation of essential oils of flowers and leaves. In flowers, the essential oil is in the epidermal cells of the petals, or in the sepals or bracts, and the oil is usually present in the upper surface of the petal.

This clinical definition leaves out a critical element of scent: the strong emotional connotations that scents have in our lives. The fresh smell of a new day, the perfume of spring flowers, the unique scent of a loved one, the heavy perfume of lilies that hangs in the warm humid summer air are all poignant "scent memories" of treasured experiences in our lives. This aspect of scent is very subjective and difficult to define or quantify, but nonetheless is a very important quality of scent to humans.

The Language of Scent

For our other senses like hearing, taste, and sight, we have a well-established vocabulary to describe them, but for the sense of smell it is frequently much more difficult for most of us to come up with definitive descriptions. Usually the most we can do is rely on similes such as, "It smells like jasmine." A report from the Howard Hughes Medical Institute titled *Seeing, Hearing and Smelling the World* (1995) states,

> Our culture places such a low value on olfaction that we have never developed a proper vocabulary for it. In *A Natural History of the Senses*, Diane Ackerman notes that it is impossible to explain how something smells to someone who hasn't smelled it. There are names for all pastels in a hue, she writes—but none for the tones and tints of smell. Nor can odors be measured on a kind of linear scale that scientists use to measure the wavelength of light or the frequency of sounds.

Some scientists have attempted to assign word descriptors to scents, with varying success. Carolus Linnaeus (1707–1778) is best known for his development of the binomial classification system used by life scientists throughout the world. Few people are aware that he also developed one of the first systems of categorizing odors. He placed them in seven groups:

- Camphoraceous
- Musky
- Floral
- Pepperminty
- Ethereal
- Pungent
- Putrid

More recently, Roman Kaiser, a fragrance and flavor chemist, in his book, *The Scent of Orchids: Olfactory, and Chemical Investigations* (1993), described four basic orchid scents according to "olfactory and chemical criteria": white-floral, rosy-floral, ionone-floral, and spicy-floral.

White-floral is the fragrance found frequently with white flowers. Most common examples include jasmine, gardenia, honeysuckle, and orange blossoms. These highly and pleasantly scented flowers are often most potent in the evening or at night and, as is commonly the case with white flowers, are night pollinated. Among orchids this group would include the genera *Aerangis*, *Angraecum*, and *Brassavola*.

The rosy-floral scent is derived from roses, specifically *Rosa centifolia*, *R. damascena*, and *R. gallica*. Other rose species, like those of Chinese descent and including many of the hybrid teas in our gardens, do not share this same scent. Among the flowers that fall in this category of scents are cyclamen, lily-of-the-valley, and sweet pea. The scents from this group are at their strongest during the day when it is sunny and warm.

The third group, the ionone-floral, is found in orange-yellow and yellow-brown flowers. It includes the heavy fragrance of freesia and *Osmanthus fragrans*. This group can cause olfactory overload so that after a few seconds of

 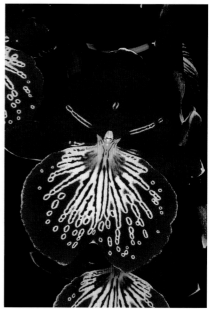

An old favorite, *Brassocattleya* Mount Hood, is typical of many white cattleya hybrids with a heady vanilla fragrance.

The gloriously colored hybrid *Miltoniopsis* (Alysen Ono × Pearl Ono) has a roselike fragrance.

inhaling flowers in this category, the perception of scent is dulled to such a degree that the nose needs to have a "time-out" before being able to accurately detect and recognize other flower scents.

The spicy-floral group is the last category and is best expressed by carnations. *Masdevallia glandulosa* is an orchid with such a scent.

The Most Fragrant Flower Colors

Genders (1977) cited an interesting study completed at the end of the nineteenth century by a French authority on scented flowers. Of the more than 4000 plants examined, white and yellow flowers accounted for more than 60 percent of all fragrant flowers, and most of the remaining fragrant flowers were colored pale pink or purple. This study further found that the order of the strength of scent or perfume by color was "white, bluish white, pale pink, mauve-pink, pale yellow, yellow, and purple; plants bearing blue, orange, red, or brown flowers have a high degree of pigmentation and generate little or no scent." While many of these generalizations hold true for the orchid family, there are exceptions. One glaring example is *Oncidium* Sharry Baby, which has a very sweetly scented dark red flower (and various other color forms).

The ease of growing and blooming combined with the luscious chocolate scent make *Oncidium* Sharry Baby one of the most popular orchids in the world.

But it is true that many of the most fragrant orchids are, indeed, white, pink, and pale yellow.

Related Plants Sometimes Have Similar Scents

Genders (1977) made another interesting observation, namely, that scents of the various genera are very much alike throughout the family. This is true, to some degree, with the orchid family. In appendix D, Orchids by Intensity of Fragrance, you will see that some of the species within the same genus do have similar fragrance descriptions.

Many people identify "orchid scent" as being the heavy sweet fragrance of the large cattleyas. This is primarily the popular belief because cattleyas were at one time the quintessential orchids sold at Mother's Day and for prom corsages for so many years. For numerous people, the only orchids they saw at florist shops were cattleyas. Very few other orchids were known or available. Now, orchids with seemingly endless varieties, shapes, colors, and scents are available from box stores to specialty orchid growers, so there is no longer any "typical orchid scent."

Fragrance Has Notes

In his humorous and very informative book, *Orchid Fever*, Eric Hansen (2000) relates how Katsuhiko Tokuda, a senior perfumer from the Japanese cosmetic company Shiseido, explains this concept.

> You have to smell through the first thing that hits your nose because this is usually the lighter aspect, often a lemony point. It is the most volatile component. The different notes or aspects reveal themselves in stages, and you have to smell through them to get to the bottom of the fragrance puzzle. If you open a bottle of perfume, what is in the neck of the bottle is what hits you first. This is the top note. Then you put the fragrance on your skin and let it evaporate for about 10 seconds, which gives you the middle ones. The base notes are the least volatile and they come up last. Use the same criteria for evaluating and understanding the scent of orchids or any other sort of flower.

When Does an Orchid Smell Its Best?

Frequently, people are disappointed when they cannot detect the fragrance of an orchid that has a reputation for its sweet scent. There are many variables in this mystery of flower fragrance, and scent can be elusive.

Some orchids smell strongest for only a few hours in the morning while others, especially the night-pollinated varieties, only yield their alluring scent in the evening. If the flowers are normally fragrant in the day, they usually reach their peak of fragrance when it is warm and in the mid part of the day. Cold, gloomy days put a damper on fragrance. If it is very humid, scent tends to hang in the air longer.

For many orchids, the maturity of the flower has some bearing on the strength of the scent, and it takes a few days after they are open before their scent can be detected. If the air is still, the fragrance is stronger than if it is gusty. Immediately after a rainfall, the oils that emit the fragrance frequently have been diluted and are thus weaker. A plant in good heath also tends to produce a stronger scent.

A primary hybrid with *Cattleya aclandiae* and *C. schilleriana* as parents, *C.* Peckhaviensis emits its strongest scent on a sunny, warm afternoon.

There can be variation even with the same species; some selections are more fragrant than others. Also, there is much variation among people regarding their individual abilities to detect different scents. And what one person will describe as a heavenly aroma, another may find repugnant.

Why Aren't Flowers as Fragrant as They Used to Be?

It is a common lament among gardeners everywhere that flowers of today don't have the heady fragrances they used to have. Genders (1977) noted that "as color (pigment) is bred into flowers, scent is usually lost." This has happened quite a bit in many horticultural arenas. It has probably been most obvious with roses and some of the old-fashioned flowers that more recently had been primarily bred for larger flower size, a wider range of flower colors, compact plant habit, increased production and vigor, and insect and disease resistance. For the most part, orchids have faced the same plight. It has not been a conspiracy by plant breeders to banish fragrance, scent has just not been a high breeding or selection priority. As a result, the other sought-after attributes won out.

Times and garden trends are changing. Rose and other flower breeders and their customers, gardeners, are showing a new appreciation for fragrance, whether they grow in outside gardens and greenhouses or in sunrooms and on windowsills. It seems that many people today, gardeners or not, are attracted to a more holistic lifestyle where it is more natural for a flower to have a pleasant fragrance. Large flower size is taking a back seat to fragrance and other desirable qualities, such as ease of growing and flowering and compact growth habit. Some orchid growers now have separate listings or notations in their catalogs or on their Web site to show which orchids are particularly fragrant. Orchid breeders are looking with a new eye (or nose) at the importance of their new hybrids having this alluring feature.

Phalaenopsis are now bred more frequently to produce fragrant results. An example is this hybrid, *Phalaenopsis* (Gelblieber-violacea × Coral Isles).

The Function of Fragrance in Orchids

As lovely and as appreciated as some orchid fragrances are by our sense of smell, their reason for being fragrant has nothing to do with us. We are just one of the inconsequential (to the plant) beneficiaries. Fragrance is an important tool that plants use to insure their survival by attracting pollinators. Lee C. Soule (1990) identified some ways that fragrance serves this function for orchids. It attracts pollinators to an important food source because fragrance is associated with liquid nectar and pollen, both of which contain highly nutritious sugars sought out by bees, hummingbirds, flies, butterflies, and other creatures. Fragrance is also a powerful sex attractant to various pollinators. We do not need the birds and the bees to tell us about this feature, as this is what the perfume industry is all about.

For detailed information on the various intriguing pollination mechanisms in orchids, readers are referred to the classic study on this topic, *Orchid Flowers: Their Pollination and Evolution* (Van der Pijl and Dodson 1969).

Fragrance in Orchids Gets New Respect

Orchids have been formally judged for 150 years, but the primary criteria used to choose award winners has been flower size, substance, color, and shape. In

Dazzling color combination and light honey fragrance make this hybrid *Miltassia* (*Brassia* Rex 'Pieper' × *Miltonia* Honolulu 'Warne's Best') a winner.

1989, the famous Japanese Prize International Orchid Show took a major step by becoming the first orchid show in the world to establish a fragrance competition for orchids. The judges were both perfume professionals and expert orchid growers. The Japanese have a long history of appreciating flowers purely for their scent. Some of the Asian *Cymbidium* species have been greatly revered for centuries for their delicate, sweet fragrance, so it seems logical that the Japanese would be pioneers in evaluating this quality in orchids.

From this show new standards for evaluating and classifying orchid scents were established. The Japanese divide orchids into two types, To-Yo-Ran (Asian cymbidiums) and Yo-Ran (Western orchids). Within each group, orchids were evaluated on four basic qualities of fragrance: intensity, gorgeousness, elegance, and freshness. What a job the judges must have had to have to quantify these qualities for all the entries!

The Greater New York Orchid Society Show of 1992 was the first show in the United States to judge orchid fragrance. Professional perfumers from Europe and Japan and American Orchid Society judges rubbed shoulders to select the orchids with the best fragrance. The show officials reported a great deal of interest from the public in this fragrance competition. Having such a prestigious orchid show place importance on fragrance demonstrates how scent in orchids is finally getting its due.

The Process of Judging Orchid Fragrance

The obstacles to judging orchid fragrance are numerous. Heading the list is the fact that scents are very personal experiences, so myriad opinions exist about what a particular orchid smells like and whether this scent is pleasant or not. Also, orchids emit their scent at different times of day or during the evening.

Linet Hamman, a director of Van Rooyen Orchids in South Africa and an accredited orchid judge, has been involved with orchid fragrance judging. Hamman (pers. comm.) states,

> The science of smelling/sniffing is quite controversial. Some people believe that you only need to whiff the air above the flower (called "head-space" by perfumers). Others suggest a waving or sniffing action, while another school believes that you have to stick your nose right into it.

Hamman explains that the South African Orchid Society has come up with a practical, simple approach to evaluate orchid fragrance. It judges on these criteria:

- Intensity. How strong is the fragrance?
- Diffuseness. Can you smell the fragrance from a distance or only very close?
- Pleasantness. How pleasant (or unpleasant) is the fragrance?
- Elegance. How well rounded and "perfumistic" is the fragrance. Chemical notes and "thin" fragrances are marked down.

All characteristics are scored on a 1-to-10 basis except for pleasantness, which is scored 1 to 20. A maximum of 50 points is possible.

Get Your Nose into Shape

In her book *The Essence of Paradise* (1991), Tovah Martin proclaimed that among humans "olfactory proficiency has taken a nosedive in the last century. We don't exercise our nose enough. And, as a result, our sense of smell has suffered."

Jochen (Joe) Heydel, a retired senior perfumer with Symrise Company and a fragrance judge for the New York International Orchid Show, says it takes five to six years of intensive odor training before a professional perfumer's nose is up to snuff (J. Heydel, pers. comm.). By this time the perfumer should be able to recognize about 3000 odors. Heydel makes constant use of his olfactory skills in everyday life. He says he experiences life in three dimensions—sight, sound, and smell—and that his nose is "always on alert."

Heydel commented that all noses are not the same and that some people naturally have a higher odor perception than others. Since he made his living with his nose, he obviously was blessed with a super nose. But he suffers from Salmon Nose Envy. He said, "Just think about how sensitive the sense of smell is for a salmon. It finds its way from the ocean to its nesting place in freshwater, hundreds or more miles solely depending on its fabulous sense of smell!"

Although few of us are blessed with a nose that is as highly perceptive and trained as is Heydel's, we can all do our part to make fragrance and smelling a more important part of our lives. The orchids in this book give you the perfect opportunity to perform painless, sweatless, sweet calisthenics with your nose. What a delightful way to work your way back to the nose fitness with which you were born.

A Word of Caution

I wish I could say that I am 100 percent certain of all the fragrance descriptions, but I am not. This subject is not pure science; much of it is anecdotal and personal opinions. We are breaking new ground with this book and I expect and welcome feedback from readers who disagree or have other opinions as to the description or intensity of the fragrance.

Chapter 2

Selecting and Buying Orchids

This is the fun part, but doing it right requires homework before you step foot in an orchid supplier's greenhouse or place an order with a mail-order company. Once this happens all reason loses out to the excitement of the moment. To buy orchids that strike your fancy, without first thinking through what fits your needs, growing requirements, and available space will frequently result in disappointing results. The orchid family is huge—in the tens of thousands! This is great in that the possibilities are vast, but the downside is that the choice can be daunting. To make the best selection you must know your preferences and consider the limitations of your growing area so you can choose orchids that will perform best under your conditions.

A super beginner's orchid, *Phalaenopsis* Orchid World 'Bonnie Vasquez' AM/AOS is a sought-after variety readily available from tissue culture. PHOTO BY ALLEN BLACK.

If you are a beginning orchid grower look over those orchids listed as being easy. As you get more confident and experienced you can try out some of the others. See appendix A, Orchids by Ease of Culture.

Light

If you have a greenhouse, you can grow all the orchids mentioned in this book; they will receive sufficient light in such a setting to grow fine. If you grow plants under lights or on a windowsill, you will be somewhat limited in your choice of plants by the lower light intensity of these situations.

While all orchids can be grown under the right light setup, especially using HID (High Intensity Discharge) lights, there still is the practical consideration of the cost of electricity. Most orchid growers who use lights choose systems with fluorescent lights because of the purchasing and operating costs. This being the case, those orchids requiring low light will do great, while those requiring medium light will do OK if they are not too tall, under 12 inches (30 cm).

For windowsill gardeners, the amount of light available for growing orchids depends upon the direction your windows face and how large they are. If you have a spacious, unobstructed south-facing window that receives at least five to six hours of sunlight, then orchids requiring high light are a possibility. For most other window exposures, the orchids preferring medium to low light intensity will be the better choice.

See appendix B, Orchids by Light Requirements, to help you choose.

Temperature

Greenhouse owners in most parts of the country find that orchids in the intermediate temperature range, 55–60°F (13–15°C) night temperature, 65–75°F (18–24°C) during the day—are the logical choice. Fortunately, most orchids in cultivation are in this category. All greenhouses have microclimates that are warmer or cooler than average. In these spots you can grow some of the orchids with warmer or cooler temperature requirements. For growers in very hot climates such as southern Texas, southern Florida, and Arizona, it is a real challenge to grow the orchids requiring cool night temperature. Without heroic efforts on the grower's part, these orchids usually suffer a slow death in such climates.

Most indoor gardeners will also find the intermediate-temperature orchids easiest to manage. If the air temperature is on the cool side, warmer orchids, like *Phalaenopsis*, can be successfully grown by placing their pots on waterproof heating pads used for seed starting. These pads increase the media and root zone temperature by 10 to 15 degrees Fahrenheit (5–8 degrees Celsius) without the cost of heating the entire growing area.

To provide lower temperatures for those orchids requiring it, windowsill growers can place the plants closer to the windows where heat is lost during the evening. Light growers using tiered carts should plant cooler loving orchids on the bottom shelf (which is also closer to the cool floor) and the warm loving ones on the top where they will benefit from the warmer air rising from the bulbs and ballasts. With HID lights the warmest area is the one closest to the bulb.

See appendix C, Orchids by Nighttime Temperature Preferences, to help you choose.

Dendrobium Aussie Quest × *Den.* Ku-Ring-Gai is an example of cold-tolerant and fragrant dendrobiums being produced by Australian orchid breeders.

Size of Plant

A large cattleya in full bloom is a spectacular sight, but whether it will fit in your growing space is an important consideration. If you are growing in a greenhouse, windowsill, or under HID lights, a large cattleya will probably fit, but how much space do you want to take up with one plant? Under fluorescent light carts, such a plant is not likely to be suitable. The plant may not fit under the light unit, and even if it does, the lower leaves will not likely receive enough light for the plant to grow and bloom well. Fortunately, breeding compact plants has become a very important criterion to orchid hybridizers today, so many of these more space efficient orchids of all types are now available.

Favorite Colors

Orchids come in such a myriad of colors, why settle for anything less than your favorite colors? When choosing orchids for color, remember that the type of light under which you view plants makes a big difference how the colors appear. All colors look accurate in diffused natural light, but regular fluorescent lights make reds pale and blues darker, and incandescent lights make reds redder and blues dull. Also, be aware that orchids will frequently not reach their true color until they have been open for several days.

Nobody ever has enough blue-flowering plants, and very few of them are fragrant, like this one, *Neostylis* Lou Sneary 'Blue Moon'. A compact grower, this orchid is perfect for lights or a windowsill.

Favorite Fragrances

Fragrance preference is very personal. A scent that may be heavenly to one person may be non-existent or nauseating to another. Check out appendix D, Orchids by Intensity of Fragrance, where fragrance descriptions are also given.

Time of Day and Year for Blooming

When are you home to enjoy your orchids? Do you work long days and rarely make it back for supper? Maybe orchids with an evening fragrance would be more rewarding for you. See appendix E, Orchids by Time of Fragrance for help in choosing your plants.

Also, what time of the year are fragrant orchids most important to you? Do you want to have a sweet-smelling orchid in your house year-round, or is winter when you would most appreciate the fragrance of flowering orchids to help you get through the winter blahs? See appendix F, Orchids by Season of Bloom, to select orchids that will put on their show when you want them to.

You will notice that some species and many of the hybrids in appendix F have a "variable" season of bloom. This includes varieties that bloom only once, but at various times of the year. Some of these varieties are triggered to initiate flower buds after they have gone through a cool drop of 15 degrees Fahrenheit (8 degrees Celsius) between daytime and evening temperatures

This cross of *Brassolaeliocattleya* Erin Kobayashi and *Potinara* Marlene Lunquist is a wonderful combination of sumptuous color and sweet fruity fragrance. It will frequently bloom more than one time a year.

or a dry period for a few to several weeks. This treatment mimics what the plants would face in their natural habitats during winter when temperatures naturally cool off or in tropical areas where plants go through a dry season. Large-scale producers of orchids like the hybrid *Phalaenopsis* can deliver blooming plants year-round by temperature manipulation. To some degree this is possible with many orchids, especially the hybrids. Some of the species adhere more to their natural biological clocks.

The Plant Selection Process

After you have worked through the exercise of deciding which orchids fit your requirements, you are now ready to shop. To find the closest orchid supplier to you, check out the American Orchid Society's marketplace on the Web (http:www.aos.org), where dealers can be searched by state. *Orchids*, the publication of the American Orchid Society, also contains ads from various orchid growers.

After you pick a grower, have arrived at the greenhouse, and have live plants in front of you, here are some things to look for. Make sure all the plants around you are healthy. If they are covered with bugs or disease, the likelihood of the plant that you pick out having them, whether you see evidence or not, is high. Assuming the plants in the greenhouse look good overall, it is time to look closely at the specific plants that interest you. Make sure they are clearly labeled. Gently lift up on the plant to see how firmly it is rooted in the pot. If it wobbles around, indicating few roots, pass it up. Notice if there are any weeds in the pot. A few cloverlike weeds, *Oxalis*, may be acceptable, but too many weeds is a sign of careless culture and these intruders will be difficult to eradicate. Since the oxalis roots wrap around the orchid's roots, the only way you can really get rid of these weeds is to repot the plant. Check out the leaves. They should be free of spots from disease and have a healthy green color.

Mature vs. Immature Plants

For the quickest, most predictable result, buy blooming-size plants. And, if you are new to orchids, you are better off purchasing a plant that is as mature as possible. If you can buy it in bloom, it is all the better. You will pay more for it, but this way you will see exactly what the flower looks like, what it smells like, how large it gets when it is mature, and it won't take as long for it to bloom again.

If you decide to buy immature plants, beware that the designations used by many growers to indicate the size or maturity of their plants—BS (blooming size) and NFS (near flowering size)—can vary quite a bit as to how long it will actually take until they flower. The usual rule of thumb is that NFS plants

What you see is what you get when you buy a mature flowering plant. This *Zygoneria* hybrid displays wild and wonderful colors and a hyacinth fragrance.

could bloom within a year; BS plants within six months. To be sure your supplier agrees with these definitions, ask him or her how long it will be before the plants bloom.

Buying Orchid Plants by Mail

Buying plants by mail is another alternative and is the only one viable for many people who live too far away for a personal visit to the grower. Fortunately, there are plenty of highly reputable orchid dealers that have excellent quality plants and know how to ship them across the country and still have them arrive at your home in top condition. I have compiled a short list of some of these reputable dealers and have annotated it with comments relevant to fragrant orchids. See appendix G, Sources for Fragrant Orchids. When you search for fragrant orchids, deal with a grower who has knowledge about and interest in these types of orchids.

To choose fragrant orchids from these vendors you can take several approaches. Some of the dealers have Web sites that allow you to do a search for fragrant orchids. Others have Web sites or catalogs where fragrance by variety is noted. Also, look for the various fragrant species mentioned in this book or hybrids that contain at least one of these species, but be aware that within a species certain selections can be much more fragrant than others. Ask the grower if his or her selection of the species you are after has a pleasant scent. Hybrids with two fragrant parents are almost certainly fragrant themselves. If only one parent is fragrant, the result is less certain. Look for specific fragrant clones that are listed in this book because they will be dependably fragrant.

Chapter 3

The Basics of Growing Orchids

Orchids have been given a bad rap. Many people still feel these plants are reserved for wealthy individuals who are endowed with a fancy greenhouse and deep pockets. While it's true that some folks spend an unimaginable amount of money on this hobby (or obsession), wealth is not a requirement. Modern production techniques have made better-quality, easier-to-grow varieties of orchids available at prices at or below what they were ten to twenty years ago. Award-quality clones can be purchased for the price of a shrub, and they are available at a variety of sources ranging from home supply stores to specialist growers. Orchids have become plants that anyone with a sunny windowsill or fluorescent light setup can afford and enjoy. They have rapidly become one of America and Europe's most popular houseplants; in fact, in the United States, they are now the second most popular blooming plant next to poinsettias! And unlike poinsettias, their popularity and sales are climbing every year.

Orchids are not difficult to grow. They just have cultural requirements that must be met, like all plants. In this chapter I will present fundamental orchid growing information, based largely on my own experience of growing orchids in a greenhouse, under lights, and in windowsills for about 40 years. Fortunately, many fine books are available on basic orchid care that you can consult for more detailed information. Check out the American Orchid Society's Web site and their bookstore for some sound advice on book selection based on your level of knowledge, what part of the country you live in, and which types of orchids you prefer to grow.

Sufficient Light

Light is one of the most critical cultural requirements for orchids as it is for all green plants. It, along with water and carbon dioxide (CO_2), are the raw material plants use to produce their food. Providing sufficient light is the cultural requirement most challenging to meet for indoor gardeners in areas of the country like New England, the Northeast, and the Midwest that suffer from short days and low light during the winter. Fortunately, plenty of species and hybrids of orchids don't require super high light intensities and so are more suited to these climates. Orchid growers blessed with naturally high light in places like Hawaii, California, and Florida have more of a problem reducing the light intensities and lowering high temperatures.

The Ins and Outs of Light Intensities

Orchids are traditionally categorized by their light requirements—high (2500 foot candles or higher), medium (1500–2500 foot candles), and low (less than 1500 foot candles). Modestly priced light meters are available to measure light in these units. All the orchids mentioned in this book are listed in appendix B by their light requirements. Most of them are in the medium light category. Those in the low to medium categories are very feasible under lights or in bright windowsills throughout the United States. From a practical point of view, the ones with high light requirements are most successfully grown in bright greenhouses.

Greenhouses collect light and are the brightest light option for growing orchids. The amount of light penetrating the greenhouse is determined by the glazing material used, the geographical location of the greenhouse, how it is sited, and whether it is shaded or not by surrounding trees or a commercial shading compound or fabric.

Windowsills also collect light, though not to the degree that greenhouses do. The amount of light that windowsills can provide is primarily determined by the size of the windows, the direction the windows face, and how far the plants are placed from the windows. The time of the year can also make a great deal of difference. During winter, for example, the sun is lower in the sky and the day length is shorter. As a result a south-facing window may be fine for certain orchids during the winter, but in summer the increased light intensity and duration of light may require moving the orchids to an east-facing window.

Artificial light sources make it possible for people without greenhouses or bright windowsills to still enjoy this hobby. Although what can be grown under these light sources is restricted only by equipment and electricity costs, growing plants under lights is a most practical method with low to medium light orchids.

The Canadian Orchid Congress published a handy chart showing the light levels offered in various growing situations. It is used here with their permission. Light levels for windowsill orchids were measured by the number of hours of sunlight offered and the direction of the window. Greenhouse light levels were expressed as a percentage of summer light to be deducted from 100 percent, the amount of light a greenhouse would receive in full sun in summer. For example, to grow an orchid requiring very high light, the last category in this chart, you would subtract 45 percent from 100 percent, leaving 55 percent. That is, an orchid requiring very high light should be grown in a greenhouse under shading with a shade density of 55 percent. Finally, light levels for plants grown under fluorescent lights were calculated in number of watts per square meter (9.84 square feet) rather than in foot candles.

Displaying tropical orchids in bloom on a plant stand indoors is a great way to chase away the winter blues. This stand backs up to an east-facing sliding glass door.

LIGHT LEVEL	WINDOWSILL & HOURS OF SUN	GREENHOUSE	FLUORESCENT LIGHTS
Low	Bright north or east facing; 1–2 hours of sun	15% of summer light	100–200 watts/meter^2
Medium	East or west facing; 2–3 hours of sun	25% of summer light	200 watts/meter^2
High	West or south facing; 4 hours of sun	35% of summer light	400 watts/meter^2
Very high	South facing; 5–6 hours of sun	45% of summer light	Not recommended

Orchids Tell You How Much Light They Need

Different types of orchids have varying light requirements since they naturally grow in a wide range of habitats. Some thrive in full sun on exposed rock, while others are at home in dense jungle shade. The leaves of the plant give you some clue as to their light requirements. Very tough, thick, stout and sometimes narrow leaves frequently are adapted to very high light intensity. Softer, more succulent, and wider leaves usually are from a lower light environment.

Although some orchid growers rely on light meters to read foot candles to determine correct light levels, the plant themselves are very good indicators. Orchids will tell you by their growth habits and leaf color if they are receiving adequate, too little, or too much light. When orchids are receiving sufficient light, the mature leaves are usually a medium to light green, the new leaves are the same size or larger and the same shape as the mature ones, the foliage is stiff and compact, not floppy, and the plants are flowering on schedule.

One of the most frequent results of inadequate light is succulent, dark green foliage and no flowers. Other symptoms include "stretching," where the distance between the new leaves on the stem of orchids like paphiopedilum, phalaenopsis, or vandas, is further apart than that of the older, mature leaves. Also, the new leaves and leads tend to be longer and thinner.

When orchids receive too much

The light yellow coloration indicates this cattleya leaf is receiving the maximum amount of light before sunburn will occur.

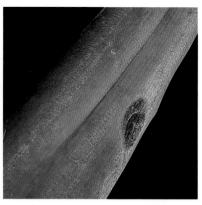

Notice that the long distance between the leaves on the stem of this paphiopedilum causes a ladder effect. This is the result of insufficient light.

A paphiopedilum leaf with a round or oval brown spot caused by too much light or sunburn.

light the leaves turn a yellow-green or take on a reddish cast and may appear stunted. In extreme cases, the leaves show circular or oval sunburn spots. The "sunburn" is actually caused by the leaf overheating and although, in itself, this leaf damage may not cause extreme harm to the plant if it is isolated to a small area, it does make the plant unsightly.

If the sunburn occurs at the growing point, it can kill that lead or the entire plant. It is possible to grow orchids under higher-than-usual light intensities if the ventilation is increased to lower the elevated leaf temperatures. Some orchid cut flower growers "push" their orchids to produce the maximum number of blooms by growing plants under the highest light intensity that does not burn them. Most hobby growers, however, want a plant that has attractive foliage and flowers and thus do not follow this practice.

Many Options with Artificial Lights

It can be rather daunting for a beginner to wade through the many lighting options available today. Fluorescent systems are still the most accessible and economical ones to buy. Three-tiered light carts are highly versatile and practical. Most of them are about 2 feet wide by 4 feet long (60 by 120 cm) so their three shelves provide 24 square feet (about 2 meters^2) of growing area. If you grow compact orchids, this will be enough space to have at least one or more orchids in bloom year-round. If you grow miniatures, it will provide space adequate for an entire collection. The convenience of such a cart can't be beat. You can place it in a heated garage, in the basement, or in a spare bedroom.

The choice of which bulbs or lamps you burn in your fixtures is a highly debated topic. Years ago the only real choices were cool white and warm white tubes. Some people still feel that a mix of half cool white and half warm white

Four-tube, rather than two-tube, units are highly recommended for low to medium light orchids.

An adjustable light fixture like this one is very handy for accommodating developing flower spikes.

tubes is the best option because they are bright and very inexpensive. With the introduction of Sylvania's Gro-Lux tubes, designed to provide light that more closely reflected the spectrum of light that plants used in photosynthesis, a new race began to produce the "best" plant bulb. The evolution of lamps has gone from Gro-Lux to wide spectrum types and now to the full spectrum bulbs. Reputedly the light cast by the full spectrum lamp most closely resembles natural sunlight. Viewed under these lamps, colors of the flowers are rendered more accurately. I have grown orchids well under all three lamp types. For growers who want flowers to appear most naturally colored under the lights and don't mind paying a premium for the lamps, the full spectrum types are the best choice. The most economical and still satisfactory pick is half warm white and half cool white lamps. A compromise between these two options would be a blend of half warm white and cool white tubes and half wide or full spectrum lamps.

Newer to the artificial light choices are the high intensity discharge (HID) lights. They are very efficient in their production of light and are especially useful for growing orchids that require higher light intensities than fluorescent lamps can provide and/or where greater working distance between the lights and plants is desired. For much more detail on this topic I recommend Charles Marden Fitch's excellent guide *Growing Orchid Under Lights* (2002) and Patti Lee's chapter in *The Gardener's Guide to Growing Orchids* (Fitch 2004b).

Some Like It Hot, Some Like It Cold

Orchids are frequently placed in three different categories based on their night temperature preferences:

Cool	45–50°F (7–10°C)
Intermediate	55–60°F (12–15°C)
Warm	65°F (18°C) and above

The assumption is that the daytime temperature will be 15 degrees Fahrenheit (8 degrees Celsius) or more warmer than this night temperature. These numbers are not absolutes, but rather guidelines. Most orchids are quite adaptable and tolerant of varying temperatures, short of freezing, but for optimum growth these temperature ranges are good targets. If orchids are exposed to cooler than recommended ranges, their growth will be slowed down and in extreme cases can lead to buds falling off before they open. Also, cooler temperatures can reduce the plant's disease resistance. A short bout of higher-than-desired temperatures will not prove harmful as long as the humidity stays high. If daytime temperatures routinely run much above those recommended, the plant will also be stressed and growth will be retarded or will stop altogether.

One critically important factor with orchids is their temperature differential requirement of at least 10 to 15 degrees Fahrenheit (5–8 degrees Celsius) between the warmer day temperature and the cooler evening temperature. If this differential is not met, the orchids will not grow vigorously, and probably most importantly, will not set flower buds. Not meeting this requirement is one of the most common reasons that home grown orchids don't bloom.

Humidity Is the Moisture in the Air

Humidity is something you can't see, but can feel on a muggy summer day or in a steamy greenhouse. Most plants, except those from arid areas, relish it. The vast majority of orchids are from the tropics where high rainfall and humidity predominate.

When plants receive ample humidity they grow lushly and their leaves have a healthy shine. Insufficient humidity can cause stunting of the growth and, in severe cases, brown tips on leaves. It can also contribute to buds falling off (bud blast), leaves wrinkling, and drying of the sheaths that can trap the buds resulting in twisted or malformed flowers.

During the winter, homes, especially those in cold climates with forced-air heating systems, have a relative humidity of about 15 percent. Since this is the average humidity found in most desert areas, something has to be done to raise the indoor humidity to 50 percent or more—the level that makes orchids and other houseplants happy. For greenhouses, this process is a relatively simple matter. Either the walkways can be regularly hosed down or foggers and commercial humidifiers can be hooked up to a humidistat so that the entire operation is automatic.

High humidity levels that are no problem in a greenhouse would peel the paint, plaster, and wallpaper off walls in a house, so home growers require a different approach. Several steps can be taken to get to the desirable humidity range without damaging results. First, it is a good idea to locate the growing area for your orchids in a naturally damp place, like the basement. Second whether or not such a location is available, the home grower will need a room humidifier. I find the best type is an evaporative-type humidifier. These units have a pad that is dampened by water in a reservoir and then a fan draws air across this pad and expels cool, humid air. Evaporative humidifiers are superior to mist type humidifiers because they don't result in a white film from the minerals in the water being deposited on leaves or furniture.

To further increase the humidity level, it is commonly recommended to grow the plants on top of a waterproof tray filled with pebbles. Water is added to the tray so that the level is just below the surface of the pebbles, then the plants are put on top of this bed of damp gravel. I don't recommend this system because I find that the pots, especially the heavy clay ones, unless they are placed on inverted saucers, quickly sink into the pebbles resulting in the media in the pots getting soggy and, after repeated waterings, the pebbles become clogged with algae and are a repository for insects and various disease organisms. An approach that works much better in my experience is to add sections of egg crate louvers, sold in home supply stores for diffusing fluorescent lights, to the trays. This material can be cut with a hack saw to whatever size you need, is rigid so will support the plants above the water, exposes more water to air so more humidity results, and is simply cleaned by removing and spraying the grating with warm water. To prevent algae or disease buildup, you can add a disinfectant like Physan to the water in the trays.

Misting is another frequently suggested method for increasing humidity. This works OK, but must be done several times a day to be effective, since the water usually evaporates very quickly. A problem with misting is that if your water source is mineral laden, your orchid's leaves may become encrusted in white to the degree that they are unsightly and light is prevented from penetrating the leaves. A side benefit to misting is that it can clean the dust from the leaves and keep down populations of pests like mites that thrive when it is hot and dry.

Orchids Need Constant Air Movement

In most tropical lands where orchids reside, they luxuriate in incessant trade winds. Air movement in a growing environment assures a more uniform air temperature and dramatically reduces disease problems by preventing the leaves from staying wet too long. It also evenly distributes the carbon dioxide that is produced by the plants in the dark and used in photosynthesis during the daylight hours.

The intention is not to create gale force winds, but to produce enough airflow to cause the leaves of the orchids to very gently sway in the breeze. I have found that two of the most effective methods to provide such an air flow for both a hobby greenhouse and an indoor growing area are the use of ceiling and oscillating fans. Ceiling fans move a huge volume of air at a low velocity in a circular pattern (from floor to ceiling or vice-versa), so they effectively prevent severe temperature stratification. They are also inexpensive, easy to install, and, if you purchase outdoor types, stand up well in moist conditions.

Oscillating fans are also a good choice, since they effectively cover large areas with a constantly changing airflow pattern without excessively drying off the plants. If you decide to go with oscillating fans, splurge for the better grade ones. Inexpensive oscillating fans have plastic gears that strip easily, so the oscillating feature won't last long.

For small hot or cold spots in the greenhouse, windowsill, or light cart, the small muffin fans frequently sold for electronic devices are efficient, quiet, and very inexpensive to operate.

The Art of Watering Orchids

Probably more orchids are killed by improper watering, usually by over watering, than by any other cultural practice. Learning how to properly water orchids is one of the most challenging aspects of orchid culture.

When I give talks about orchids, one of the first questions asked by those attending is, "How often should I water my orchids?" I really wish there was an easy answer to this question, but there is not. There are so many variables involved! Here are just a few of them:

- Are you growing in plastic or clay pots? The medium in plastic pots dries off much slower than it does in clay. With plastic, the medium dries out from the top down, so although it may be dry on top, it may still be damp 1 inch (2.5 cm) below the surface. With clay pots, the medium dries out more uniformly because the pot is porous.
- What type of media are you using? Media vary dramatically on how much water they retain. For instance, sphagnum moss usually stays wet much longer than bark.
- Is the orchid pot bound or not? An overgrown orchid will dry off much more quickly than one that has plenty of space in the pot.
- What is your growing environment? Is it high humidity or low? Plants and media in low humidity dry off quicker. What temperature are your plants growing in? Warmer temperatures increase water evaporation. How much ventilation do your plants have? The more ventilation, especially if air is vented to the outside, the quicker water in the media evaporates.
- Are the orchids actively growing or dormant? When species of certain orchids like some of the dendrobiums and catasetums are going through their winter rest period, they need and should only be given very little water, but when they start active growth in the spring and summer they require copious amounts of water.
- What type of orchid are you growing? Some, like cattleyas, like to get dry between waterings; others like paphiopedilums, phalaenopsis, and miltonias prefer to always be damp.
- How old is the orchid growing medium? Anyone who has repotted an orchid in fresh fir bark knows that the plant has to be watered much more frequently the first few weeks until the medium gets properly wetted. As this bark gets older it retains water longer. That's true for most media.

You can now see why this is not an easy question to answer without considering many different factors.

Watering Techniques

Taking all of the above in consideration, you need to make the decision when and how much to water. I find the pot weighing method one of the easiest to learn. This first involves very thoroughly watering the orchid in its pot. Then "weigh" it by picking it up. Now you know what it feels like when it is saturated with water. Wait a day or so and weigh it again by picking it up. Feel the difference in the weight as the medium becomes drier. Keep doing this each day until you judge, by looking at the surface and sticking your finger into the top 1 inch (2.5 cm) or so of the medium and knowing whether this orchid prefers to be on the damp or dry side, that it is time to water. Note what the weight is now. Then water thoroughly. This entire process sounds tedious, but you will be amazed how quickly you catch on. Once you master it, you will always know the right time to water. Just lift the pot and you will get your answer.

Here are some other watering tips:

- Grow plants of similar type, media, pot type, and sizes in the same area. This will make watering them easier, since they will have very similar moisture requirements.
- Water with warm water. Very cold water can cause root and bud shock.
- Always use a water breaker, or for only a few plants, a sprinkling can with a long spout and a water diffusing rose. These instruments water plants thoroughly without washing out the media. A huge selection of watering wands is offered now. I really like the ones with multiple settings on the head that allow you to drench or mist without changing attachments, and I find that those equipped with a finger trigger make it easier to regulate the flow of water than those with an on-and-off valve.
- Never let the water breaker or the end of the hose touch the ground. This was a commandment given to me by my first horticulture professor, D. C. Kiplinger. He preached that floors and soil are where the pathogens hang out and a hose can be an all too effective way of spreading them.
- When you water, water thoroughly. The water should pour out from the bottom of the pot. This method of watering ensures that the media is saturated and flushes out any excessive fertilizer salts.
- Never let an orchid pot sit in water for any length of time. If the pot has a saucer, make sure to keep the saucer free of water. Excess standing water will prematurely rot the media and roots and will be a source of accumulating fertilizer salts and pathogens.
- Water the plants early in the day or afternoon when there is adequate time for the foliage to dry off before nightfall. Wet foliage in the evening is an invitation for disease.

Signs of Improper Watering—Roots Tell the Story

Unfortunately, over and under watering result in many of the same symptoms because the net effect of both practices is the same, damaged or destroyed root systems, which results in dehydration of the plant. The signs of this problem can be pleated leaves on miltonias, excessively shriveled pseudobulbs on cattleyas, yellow and wilted bottom leaves on phalaenopsis, and bud blast (buds fall off instead of opening) on all orchids.

To better evaluate whether over or under watering has caused these symptoms, you must remove the plant from its pot. Many beginner growers are reluctant to do this, but if done carefully it will not harm plants and it is an absolutely necessary procedure to see what is going on with the root system. When the plant is removed from the pot, check out the medium. Is it soggy? Does it have a bad (rotting) smell? Are the roots dark and mushy? These are all signs of over watering. If the roots are dry rather than succulent, and have no or few growing root tips, the orchid probably has not received enough water. This can be because the media is too coarse and thus makes poor contact with the roots or the water was not applied frequently enough.

The remedy to this situation depends on how dire the root condition of the plant is. If there are still healthy, firm roots, then cut off all the soft ones with a sterile tool like a single-edged razor, and repot in new mix. Water lightly for a few weeks to encourage new root development. Mist the plants a few times a day to prevent the leaves from drying out.

If the roots are almost all gone, emergency measures are called for and recovery is not definite. Cut off all the dead or damaged roots, then drench the roots with a liquid rooting hormone like Dip 'n Grow. Allow this liquid hormone to dry on the roots for about an hour, then repot the orchid in fresh media that has been pre-dampened. Don't water for a day, then water once and place the potted orchid in an enclosed terrarium (like a High Top Propagator or an empty aquarium) with damp sphagnum moss or pebbles on the bottom. Close the top and put the terrarium in a location with diffused light. In a greenhouse, this would be a shady spot with no direct sunlight; under lights, this would be at the ends of the tubes where there is less illumination. If the terrarium is in the cool part of the greenhouse or growing area, put the entire terrarium on

Enclosed containers like this High Top Propagator provide an atmosphere of 100-percent humidity in which plants with damaged roots can reroot themselves.

a heating mat set for 70°F (21°C) to provide bottom heat to stimulate rooting. If disease is a concern, spray the orchid leaves with a disinfectant solution like Physan. In this environment of 100-percent humidity the leaves will not dehydrate, so there will be no stress on the orchid while it reroots itself. Water the media only when it gets dry, keep the gravel or moss in the bottom of the terrarium damp, and leave the plant enclosed until new root growth is very apparent. This may take a few months. There are no guarantees with this method, but it has brought back several orchids for me that were in the "hopeless" category.

Fertilizing Is Not a Cure-All

Many people put much too much faith in fertilizers. They think fertilizer is some type of elixir that will save the day. Actually, if the plant is in poor health, fertilizers are rarely the answer. In fact, if the roots are damaged, as is frequently the case, applying fertilizers worsens the problem. If roots are not functioning well, they cannot absorb the fertilizer, and the fertilizer that is not used by the plant can accumulate in the orchid media. This buildup of fertilizer salts can further dehydrate and damage the remaining roots. Fertilizers are most useful as a boost to help an already healthy plant grow better.

The number and types of fertilizers on the market can make your head spin! There is much mumbo-jumbo about why one fertilizer is better than another. Fortunately, the choice is not near as complicated as some manufacturers seem to make it. The most enlightening and cogent explanation of orchid fertilization that I have read appeared in *Orchids* in an article titled "Without High Phosphorous, A New Fertilizer Proves Itself with Orchids" by Jan Szyren (2003) and the accompanying sidebar by Bill Argo from the Horticulture Department at Michigan State University. According to Szyren, orchids, like all plants, need a balanced fertilizer, but they do have some special requirements. A good water-soluble fertilizer, the kind most recommended and used by orchid growers, should have various qualities. From this article and my own experience, I believe the following criteria apply to fertilizers for most orchid growing situations:

- Nitrogen should be provided as nitrate and ammonia. Both forms are more immediately available to orchids in warm and cool temperatures and do not have to be broken down by soil organisms before they become available, which is what is required with urea-based products.
- High amounts of nitrogen, much more than 20 percent, are not necessary to grow the best plants no matter what media they are grown in. Too much of any nutrient cannot be used by the orchid plant and, as a result, merely ends up as a pollutant.

- A high-phosphorous fertilizer (sometimes called "bloom booster") is not necessary to trigger better blooming.
- For most water sources a fertilizer with supplementary calcium (up to 15 percent) and magnesium (up to 8 percent) is a real plus. Get a water test to find out if you happen to have sufficient quantities of either of these so that they don't need to be included in the fertilizer that you use.
- For most water sources, trace amounts of sodium, manganese, copper, zinc, boron, iron, and molybdenum are beneficial.

The article mostly discusses two special orchid fertilizers developed for orchids, one formulated for the well water at Michigan State University and another for "pure" water. Although I have tried and am still using the "pure" water formulation with good results, other fertilizers on the market also have these qualities.

Other pointers to keep in mind are that it is better to fertilize more frequently at a more dilute rate that less often at a higher concentration. Follow the recommendations on the fertilizer container regarding how much to use. When in doubt apply less, not more fertilizer. If you apply fertilizer at higher-than-recommended dosage, root burn can occur. Remember fertilizers are a form of salt and salts were some of the earliest weed killers, so they will damage plants at high concentrations. Also, to be on the safe side, be sure your media is damp before applying fertilizer. It is a good practice to drench the media every few weeks or so with fresh water that contains no nutrients to wash out any excess fertilizer salts. This is called "leaching."

Pots, Potting, and Potting Media

Plastic pots have replaced clay as the standard. They are lightweight, inexpensive, available in a vast range of sizes and types, and do not break easily. For orchids that prefer constant moisture, they are almost always the choice. Clay pots do still have a place, though. Their advantages include that they dry off very thoroughly; are heavier, which can be a bonus for top-heavy orchids; and are easier to use with clamp-on supports and clips, since clay pots are more rigid than plastic. All of these features make them favored by some growers. The truth is, you can grow most orchids in either type of pot, as long as you learn the watering characteristics of each.

Orchids can also be mounted on wood or cork, a growing method often recommended for plants that resent frequent potting and grow naturally as epiphytes in situations where their roots are accustomed to being exposed to the air. Orchids that require excellent drainage and those with downward-growing flower spikes, like stanhopeas, do well in slatted wooden baskets.

The range of choices in potting media is overwhelming and the ratios of

When an epiphytic orchid like this cattleya runs out of room, new roots and leads form outside of the pot. It would have been best to repot this orchid just as new roots are forming rather than after they have already fully developed. In this case the roots will need to be trimmed before placing into a new pot.

what materials are combined to give just the right potting media are just as varied as everyone's favorite recipe for brownies. Most all of them will work OK, but each has its good and bad features. Here are some considerations and generalizations regarding orchid potting and potting media:

- Determine whether your orchid is a terrestrial or epiphyte. Terrestrials do better in a heavy, moisture-retaining mix, while epiphytes require excellent drainage.
- Know your watering habits. If you water frequently, use a more free draining mix, one that contains larger grades of bark, coco chunks, charcoal, or Aliflor. If you water less often, choose a media that retains more water, such as sphagnum moss or a finer grade of bark, coco chunks, or charcoal.
- Use fine media for orchids with smaller roots, larger media for orchids with larger roots.
- Remember that the frequency of repotting varies from eight months to two years depending on how often you water, how quickly the orchid outgrows its space, and the type of media used.
- Keep in mind that the best time to repot orchids is when they are putting out new roots. This is usually immediately after they bloom.
- When repotting, remove all dead or shriveled growths and roots with a sterile knife. A disposable single-edged razor blade is perfect for this. Use one blade per plant to prevent disease spread.

Insect and Disease Control—Think Least-Toxic Solution

Fortunately, orchids have relatively few pest problems. Prevention is the key, so isolate new orchids purchased for at least three weeks. Routinely examine the young developing leaves, especially their undersides, and the flower buds because insects are always attracted to succulent new growth. When you find any insect pests, eliminate them immediately. This can be done most simply by washing them off with warm water. I frequently follow this up with a spray of insecticidal soap, light horticultural oil, or neem. One of my newest favorite general insect controls is OrangeGuard, which is basically orange oil. It's food-safe; effective on all soft-bodied insects like aphids, scale, and mealy bugs; and smells great. If you stay on top of insect control in the early stages, you will rarely have to resort to the more toxic petrochemical choices.

It is basically the same story for diseases. Keep your growing operation clean and you will greatly reduce your disease problems. Again isolate new plants, water only during the day and afternoon so the foliage dries by the evening, be sure you have good air circulation, and use sterile tools when performing any cutting. If you discover a portion of a leaf with a suspicious spot, remove the affected portion with a new single-edged razor or sharp shears that have been flame sterilized. Cut the leaf back to at least $1/2$ inch (1.5 cm) of healthy tissue, and then spray the plant with a general disinfectant like Physan. Some growers have successfully treated cuts with cinnamon.

For much more detail on this subject, I highly recommend the superb American Orchid Society booklet titled *Orchid Pests and Diseases* (Watson 2002).

Summer Care

Some orchid growers continue growing their plants indoors under lights, in windowsills, or in the greenhouse throughout the summer. The challenge during this time is to reduce the light intensity and control the high heat, both

Vandaceous plants can easily be summered over outdoors by hanging them from a free-standing support or suspended rod against the garage.

The author's shade house is an 8-foot (2.4-meter) square simply constructed structure using wood lath and 4- x 4-inch (10- x 10-cm) pressure treated wood posts.

Inside the shade house plants are arranged on stepped wire benches to allow easy watering, good air circulation, and adequate water drainage.

of which can be damaging. For these reasons, summering the orchids out-doors is an attractive option. For growers who rely on lights, moving plants outdoors means a welcome relief from high electric bills and for greenhouse and windowsill growers it provides an opportunity to clean up the growing area. Also, most orchids are not in bloom during the summer so they are not at their best visually and they respond very favorably to a summer vacation outdoors. I summer my orchids in a lath house constructed of pressure-treated wood supports and lath.

Shading, usually 50–60 percent or more depending on the location of the shade house and the types of orchids grown, is very necessary and is provided by lath or shading fabrics. I also installed in this shade house a watering sys-tem consisting of multiple small sprayers or misters controlled by a timer that has a manual override. I grow the plants on stepped wire frame benches that ensure even lighting and easy watering.

I covered the roof of the lath house with 6-mil clear plastic, which is stretched over a peaked wooden frame. I used to leave the roof of the lath house open to receive natural rainfall, but found that it sometimes rained when I didn't want it to, at night, when it was too cool or when it was already wet. The covered roof gives me control to water when it is needed. Besides pro-viding an opportunity to clean up your indoor growing area, having a space outdoors allows you to apply heavier duty pest controls, if necessary, without smelling up your house. Finally, the natural temperature differential between day and night, especially in the early fall, is very effective in setting flower buds for the upcoming late fall and winter blooming.

Chapter 4

The Cattleya Alliance

To many people, especially those from the older generation, the words *orchid* and *cattleya* were synonymous. The first prom or Mother's Day corsage that they gave or received was likely purple. In fact the color "orchid" is this purple hue.

The Cattleya Alliance has long been a favorite of both professional and amateur orchid growers worldwide because it has one of the widest spectrums of rich colors and is found with growth habits ranging from miniature to 3 feet (90 cm) or more. Sweet, heavy fragrance has also frequently been a trademark of some of the species and many of the hybrids in this group.

Most genera within this illustrious group, including *Brassavola*, *Encyclia*, *Epidendrum*, and *Rhyncholaelia*, can be interbred to produce a seemingly endless array of color and fragrance combinations.

Since the first cattleya hybrids were made in the mid 1800s by the famous English company, Veitch Nurseries, breeders have kept up a furious pace of new introductions with no end in sight. Before cloning made award-quality plants affordable, the best forms and hybrids commanded sky-high prices. Today's hobbyist growers are treated to the finest quality hybrids and clones at very reasonable prices, and these plants are easier to grow.

Earlier hybridizing efforts, as was the case with many other garden flowers, particularly roses, were primarily focused on producing bigger and more numerous flowers per stem in a broader range of colors with more vigorous plants. Little or no effort was made to retain fragrance in these hybrids. Since fragrance can be a recessive characteristic, the result was that fewer hybrids retained this most desirable quality. Fortunately, orchid buyers have been clamoring for the sweet scent of many of the species, and so breeders are responding with efforts to bring back fragrance in many of today's hybrids.

In this chapter I present profiles of some of key members of the Cattleya Alliance, starting with the species, followed by the hybrids. Standard-sized cattleya hybrids grow 12–18 inches (30–45 cm) on average, but can get larger. Minicatts (dwarf and miniature cattleya hybrids) range from less than 6 inches (15 cm) to more than 12 inches (30 cm).

Species

Brassavola flagellaris
PRONUNCIATION: bra-SAH-vo-la

ORIGIN: Brazil

DESCRIPTION AND QUALITIES: Produces one of the most pleasing fragrances of all the orchids.

INTENSITY OF FRAGRANCE: Very strong

WHEN FRAGRANT: Evening

DESCRIPTION OF FRAGRANCE: Hot-chocolate

FLOWER DESCRIPTION: Creamy green petals and sepals with white heart-shaped lip and a green-yellow throat. Flowers less than 3 inches (7.5 cm) wide. Inflorescence 3–5 inches (7.5–12.5 cm) tall, bearing three to five flowers.

SEASON OF BLOOM: Fall

MATURE PLANT: Skinny, fleshy, semi-pendulous, terete leaves up to 18 inches (45 cm) long.

EASE OF CULTURE: Intermediate

SUITABLE GROWING AREA: Windowsill, greenhouse

LIGHT: High to full sun

Brassavola flagellaris is very fragrant yet not commonly grown. PHOTO BY ALLEN BLACK.

Temperature: Intermediate to warm

Recommended potting medium: A clay pot or wooden basket supplemented with chunks of cork

Brassavola nodosa

Pronunciation: bra-SAH-vo-la

Aka: *Epidendrum nodosum, Brassavola venosa*

Origin: Mexico, Central America, Columbia, Venezuela

Common name: Lady of the night

Fragrant offspring: *Brassavola* Moonlight Perfume (*B. nodosa* × *B. glauca*)

Description and qualities: This very popular native of Mexico and South America is very easy to grow and bloom.

Intensity of fragrance: Strong

When fragrant: Evening

Description of fragrance: Freesia, lily-of-the-valley

Flower description: Pale green to creamy white flowers with lips sometimes marked purple. Flowers 3–6 inches (7.5–15 cm) across. Inflorescence erect, 8 inches (20 cm) tall, bearing one to six flowers.

Season of bloom: Variable

Mature plant: Clump forming, to 18 inches (45 cm) tall but usually much shorter. Stems and leaves are subterete.

Ease of culture: Easy

Suitable growing area: Windowsill, lights, greenhouse

Light: Medium to high

A wonderful beginner's orchid, *Brassavola nodosa* fills up the evening air with its enchanting scent.

TEMPERATURE: Intermediate to warm

RECOMMENDED POTTING MEDIUM: Fine- to medium-textured, well-drained mix.

SPECIAL CULTURAL TIP: Don't divide unnecessarily as this orchid flowers and looks best when grown into a large specimen plant.

COMMENT: This species frequently passes on its ease of blooming, compact habit, and fragrance to its offspring.

OTHER FRAGRANT BRASSAVOLAS: *B. cucullata*—musty-soapy; *B.* Little Stars— soapy-sweet; *B. martiana*—soapy-sweet; *B. tuberculata*—nicotiana, gardenia; *B.* Yaki 'Black's Best'—musty-soapy.

Cattleya bicolor var. *grossii*

PRONUNCIATION: KAT-lee-a

AKA: *Cattleya grossii, Epidendrum iridee, Epidendrum bicolor*

ORIGIN: Brazil

COMMON NAME: Bi-colored cattleya

DESCRIPTION AND QUALITIES: A handsome, scented variety that is not common in today's collections.

INTENSITY OF FRAGRANCE: Light

WHEN FRAGRANT: Day

DESCRIPTION OF FRAGRANCE: Spicy, aromatic floral, rose

FLOWER DESCRIPTION: Coppery to pinkish brown flowers with striking dark pink lips. Flowers 3 inches (7.5 cm) wide. Inflorescence terminal, 8–10 inches (20–35 cm) long, bearing up to 10 flowers.

SEASON OF BLOOM: Fall

MATURE PLANT: Slender pseudobulbs grow to 20 to 36 inches (50–85 cm) tall.

EASE OF CULTURE: Intermediate

SUITABLE GROWING AREA: Windowsill, greenhouse

LIGHT: Medium to high

TEMPERATURE: Intermediate

RECOMMENDED POTTING MEDIUM: Medium-textured, well-drained mix

SPECIAL CULTURAL TIP: Repot only when new roots are starting to develop.

COMMENT: Introduced by Messrs. Loddiges of England in 1838 after it was collected from Brazil.

A waxy dark flower with a contrasting bright pink lip makes *Cattleya bicolor* var. *grossii* a stunner.

Cattleya guttata

PRONUNCIATION: KAT-lee-a

AKA: *Epidendrum elegans, Cattleya elatior*

ORIGIN: Brazil

COMMON NAME: Spotted cattleya

DESCRIPTION AND QUALITIES: A spectacular addition to any collection.

INTENSITY OF FRAGRANCE: Light

WHEN FRAGRANT: Day

DESCRIPTION OF FRAGRANCE: Sweet floral

FLOWER DESCRIPTION: Waxy green flowers with purple spots. The top portion of the lip is white while the bottom is purple. Flowers 2–3 inches (5–7.5 cm) wide. Inflorescence up to 18 inches (45 cm) tall, bearing five to six flowers.

SEASON OF BLOOM: Summer to fall

MATURE PLANT: Medium-sized grower to 24 to 40 inches (60–100 cm) tall.

EASE OF CULTURE: Intermediate

SUITABLE GROWING AREA: Windowsill, greenhouse

LIGHT: Medium to high

TEMPERATURE: Intermediate to warm

RECOMMENDED POTTING MEDIUM: Medium-textured cattleya mix

SPECIAL CULTURAL TIP: Repot only when new roots are forming.

COMMENT: First collected by Portuguese botanist José Vellozo in Brazil in 1790.

Nature has a way of being dramatic, as *Cattleya guttata* with its flamboyant flowers illustrates.

Cattleya intermedia

PRONUNCIATION: KAT-lee-a

AKA: *Cattleya ovata, Cattleya maritima*

ORIGIN: Brazil

COMMON NAME: Intermediate cattleya

DESCRIPTION AND QUALITIES: This species, which is easy to grow and bloom, has many color forms, including 'Carlos', a selected cultivar with a floral fragrance.

INTENSITY OF FRAGRANCE: Strong

WHEN FRAGRANT: Day

DESCRIPTION OF FRAGRANCE: Sweet floral

FLOWER DESCRIPTION: White to pale purple flowers up to 6 inches (15 cm) wide. Inflorescence 10 in. (25 cm) long, with few to several flowers.

SEASON OF BLOOM: Variable

MATURE PLANT: Stems can reach about 15 inches (40 cm) and leaves about 6 inches (15 cm) long.

EASE OF CULTURE: Intermediate

SUITABLE GROWING AREA: Windowsill, greenhouse

LIGHT: Medium to high

TEMPERATURE: Intermediate

RECOMMENDED POTTING MEDIUM: Medium-textured orchid mix

COMMENT: Introduced in 1824 by Captain Graham and first grown at the Glasgow Botanic Garden in Scotland.

Cattleya maxima

PRONUNCIATION: KAT-lee-a

AKA: *Epidendrum maximum*

ORIGIN: Ecuador, Colombia, Peru

DESCRIPTION AND QUALITIES: Considered one of Ecuador's most beautiful orchids.

INTENSITY OF FRAGRANCE: Strong

Cattleya intermedia var. *orlata* has an arresting purple lip that contrasts with its light pink petals and sepals.

An exceptional selection of the species, *Cattleya maxima* 'Mountainside' is from the Vermont orchid growing establishment, Mountain Orchids.

WHEN FRAGRANT: Day

DESCRIPTION OF FRAGRANCE: Heliotrope, sweet pea

FLOWER DESCRIPTION: Lavender-pink flowers with dark purple veins in the lips and yellow throats. Flowers 5 inches (12.7 cm) wide. Inflorescence up to 12 inches (30 cm) tall, bearing flowers in groups of three or more.

SEASON OF BLOOM: Summer to fall

MATURE PLANT: Reaches 5 to 15 inches (12.5–45 cm) tall.

EASE OF CULTURE: Intermediate

SUITABLE GROWING AREA: Windowsill, greenhouse

LIGHT: Medium to high

TEMPERATURE: Intermediate

RECOMMENDED POTTING MEDIUM: Medium-textured bark or coco chunk mix

COMMENT: Discovered by Hipólito Ruíz López and José A. Pavon, Spanish botanists in 1777 in the Peruvian Andes.

Cattleya walkeriana var. *alba*

PRONUNCIATION: KAT-lee-a

AKA: *Cattleya bulbosa*

ORIGIN: Brazil

COMMON NAME: Walker's cattleya

FRAGRANT OFFSPRING: *Laeliocattleya* Mini Purple (*Cattleya walkeriana* × *Laelia pumila*)

A white form of the species, *Cattleya walkeriana* var. *alba* has fine shape and super fragrance. It is used extensively in breeding because of both characteristics..

DESCRIPTION AND QUALITIES: The species is found in various color forms with the white-flowering ones usually having the best shape.

INTENSITY OF FRAGRANCE: Strong

WHEN FRAGRANT: Day

DESCRIPTION OF FRAGRANCE: Vanilla, cinnamon

FLOWER DESCRIPTION: White, flat flowers of a waxy, thick substance. Flower 3 inches (7.5 cm) across. Inflorescence 8 inches (20 cm) long, bearing one to a few flowers. The typical species has rose-purple flowers.

SEASON OF BLOOM: Variable

MATURE PLANT: A miniature grower, up to about 6 inches (15 cm) tall.

EASE OF CULTURE: Intermediate

SUITABLE GROWING AREA: Windowsill, lights, greenhouse

LIGHT: Medium to high

TEMPERATURE: Intermediate

RECOMMENDED POTTING MEDIUM: Medium orchid mix

COMMENT: An easy-to-grow and popular species. The compact habit and fragrance of this species have made it a cornerstone in miniature cattleya breeding. Discovered by Mr. Gander in Brazil in 1839.

Encyclia cordigera

PRONUNCIATION: en-SIK-lee-a

AKA: *Encyclia atropurpurea*

ORIGIN: Central America, Columbia, Venezuela, Mexico

DESCRIPTION AND QUALITIES: Considered by many to be the handsomest Mexican encyclia. Has many color forms. Produces its strongest fragrance in full sunlight.

INTENSITY OF FRAGRANCE: Strong

WHEN FRAGRANT: Day

DESCRIPTION OF FRAGRANCE: Honey and vanilla

FLOWER DESCRIPTION: Deep maroon-red flowers with bright pink lips. Flowers about 3 inches (7.5 cm) wide. Inflorescence 24 inches (60 cm) tall, bearing 2 to 10 flowers.

SEASON OF BLOOM: Variable

MATURE PLANT: Clusters of fat, oblong pseudobulbs grow 12–15 inches (30-37 cm) tall.

Vanilla fragrance and easy culture make *Encyclia cordigera* a favorite with beginners and veteran orchid growers.

EASE OF CULTURE: Intermediate
SUITABLE GROWING AREA: Windowsill, greenhouse
LIGHT: Medium to high
TEMPERATURE: Intermediate to warm
RECOMMENDED POTTING MEDIUM: Standard cattleya mix
COMMENT: Described by F. H. A. von Humboldt in 1815 as *Cymbidium cordigerum.*

Encyclia fragrans

PRONUNCIATION: en-SIK-lee-a
AKA: *Epidendrum fragrans*
ORIGIN: Mexico, Central America, northern South America
COMMON NAME: Clamshell orchid
DESCRIPTION AND QUALITIES: A cockle-shell orchid that is simple to grow.
INTENSITY OF FRAGRANCE: Strong
WHEN FRAGRANT: Day
DESCRIPTION OF FRAGRANCE: Honey, vanilla, gardenia, magnolia, lilac
FLOWER DESCRIPTION: Greenish white sepals and petals with purple stripes in the lip. Flowers 2 inches (5 cm) across. Inflorescence to 5 inches (13 cm) long, bearing two to eight flowers.
SEASON OF BLOOM: Variable
MATURE PLANT: Reaches up to 16 inches (40 cm) tall.
EASE OF CULTURE: Easy

The flower of *Encyclia fragrans* may not be that impressive, but its heavy gardenia fragrance is.

Suitable growing area: Windowsill, greenhouse
Light: Medium
Temperature: Intermediate
Recommended potting medium: Standard cattleya mix
Comment: A great beginner's orchid because of its undemanding culture. One of the earliest orchids in cultivation, it flowered at the Royal Botanic Gardens, Kew, in England in 1782.
Other fragrant encyclias: *Encycl. adenocaula*—floral; *Encycl. citrina*—lemon; *Encycl. lancifolia*—spicy; *Encycl. phoenicea*—chocolate; *Encycl. polybulbon*—sandalwood, cloves; *Encycl. radiata*—spicy floral, coconut cream pie, lilac, carnation, hyacinth; *Encycl. tampensis*—honey; *Encycl. trulla*—spice.

Laelia anceps

Pronunciation: LAY-lee-a
Aka: *Laelia barkeriana*
Origin: Mexico
Common name: El Toro
Description and qualities: This species comes in many color forms.
Intensity of fragrance: Light
When fragrant: Day
Description of fragrance: Primrose, vanilla
Flower description: Light lavender flowers with darker purple lips and throats. Flowers 2.5–3 inches (6–8 cm) wide. Inflorescence a tall spike up to 3 feet (1 m) long, bearing flowers in clusters of two to six.
Season of bloom: Fall
Mature plant: A compact plant about 1 foot (30 cm) tall.
Ease of culture: Easy
Suitable growing area: Greenhouse, windowsill
Light: Medium to high
Temperature: Intermediate
Recommended potting medium: Well-drained cattleya mix or mounted
Comment: A hardy orchid to 20°F (–6°C) that is sometimes planted outdoors in parts of Florida and California. First introduced by Messrs. Loddiges in 1835.

Laelia anceps comes in many color forms. This especially fine selection in the photo comes from J & L Orchids in Connecticut.

Laelia perrinii

PRONUNCIATION: LAY-lee-a

AKA: *Cattleya perrinii, Cattleya intermedia* var. *angustifolia*

ORIGIN: Central Brazil

COMMON NAME: Perrin's laelia

DESCRIPTION AND QUALITIES: A compact grower not yet commonly grown.

INTENSITY OF FRAGRANCE: Light

WHEN FRAGRANT: Day

DESCRIPTION OF FRAGRANCE: Spicy floral

FLOWER DESCRIPTION: Lavender flowers with deep violet-edged trumpet-shaped lips and with white throats. Flowers up to 6 inches (15 cm) wide. Inflorescence 3–6 inches (7–15 cm), bearing one to four flowers. The species has several color forms including a white (*alba*) and a blue (*coerulea*).

SEASON OF BLOOM: Fall

MATURE PLANT: Reaches about 6 inches (15 cm) high.

EASE OF CULTURE: Easy

SUITABLE GROWING AREA: Windowsill, greenhouse

LIGHT: Medium to high

TEMPERATURE: Intermediate

RECOMMENDED POTTING MEDIUM: Medium-textured epiphytic mix

SPECIAL CULTURAL TIP: Prefers warm, wet summers and cooler, drier winters.

COMMENT: Described by botanist James Bateman in 1847, who named it after a Mr. Perrin, gardener for R. Harrison.

A compact grower and not yet commonly grown, *Laelia perrinii* has a light, spicy, pleasant scent.

Laelia tenebrosa

PRONUNCIATION: LAY-lee-a

AKA: *Laelia grandis* var. *tenebrosa*

ORIGIN: Brazil

COMMON NAME: Dark laelia

DESCRIPTION AND QUALITIES: This laelia species displays a very wide range of rich, bright colors in its flowers, from yellow to orange and shades of red. The lip is also variable in color, but always striking.

INTENSITY OF FRAGRANCE: Light

WHEN FRAGRANT: Day

DESCRIPTION OF FRAGRANCE: Spicy

FLOWER DESCRIPTION: Bronze- or copper-colored flowers, lips trumpet-like and flaring, white with a purple ring. Flowers up to about 7 inches (18 cm) wide. Inflorescence about 12 inches (30 cm) long, bearing two or three flowers that last about two weeks.

SEASON OF BLOOM: Summer to fall

MATURE PLANT: Reaches about 18 inches (45 cm) tall. Leaves sometimes have a purplish tint.

EASE OF CULTURE: Challenging

SUITABLE GROWING AREA: Windowsill, greenhouse

LIGHT: Medium to high

TEMPERATURE: Intermediate

RECOMMENDED POTTING MEDIUM: Coarse-textured, fast-draining mix

Laelia tenebrosa displays a dazzling color combination that only nature could have imagined.

SPECIAL CULTURAL TIP: Water heavily during the growing season, but keep on the dry side for about three months during the winter. Increase light intensity to initiate flowering.

COMMENT: Described in *Orchid Review* in 1893 by Robert A. Rolfe.

OTHER FRAGRANT LAELIAS: *L. albida*—primrose; *L. lundii*—floral scent; *L. pumila* var. *coerulea*—light floral; *L. purpurata* var. *werckhauseri*—spice, anise; *L. rubescens*—wintergreen.

Rhyncholaelia digbyana

PRONUNCIATION: rink-oh-LAY-lee-a

AKA: *Brassavola digbyana, Laelia digbyana*

ORIGIN: Mexico, Belize, Guatemala, Honduras

FRAGRANT OFFSPRING: *Brassolaeliocattleya* Ports of Paradise (*Brassolaeliocattleya* Fortune × *Rhyncholaelia digbyana*)

DESCRIPTION AND QUALITIES: Very important as a parent to impart its wonderful fragrance, fringed lip, and large flower size. Ernest Hetherington (1986a) of Fred E. Stewart Orchids stated, "The delightful fragrance blends with other species, such as *Cattleya dowiana*, into a multitude of pleasing fragrances."

INTENSITY OF FRAGRANCE: Strong

WHEN FRAGRANT: Evening

DESCRIPTION OF FRAGRANCE: Lily-of-the-valley, lemon

FLOWER DESCRIPTION: Apple green flowers with spectacular, unique, fringed lips. Flowers usually 4–5 inches (10–13 cm) across, but can be

Rhyncholaelia digbyana has passed on its unique fringed lip, lime-colored flower, and sumptuous fragrance to many modern hybrids.

up to 7 inches (18 cm). Inflorescence 3–6 inches (7.5–15 cm) tall, bearing one flower.

SEASON OF BLOOM: Spring to summer

MATURE PLANT: Compact habit, up to 14 inches (40 cm) tall.

EASE OF CULTURE: Challenging

SUITABLE GROWING AREA: Windowsill, greenhouse

LIGHT: Medium to high

TEMPERATURE: Intermediate

RECOMMENDED POTTING MEDIUM: Mounted on a slab or in very loose, well-draining medium in a clay pot

SPECIAL CULTURAL TIP: Keep dry and on the very bright side. Allow plants to dry out well between waterings.

COMMENT: Named after Vincent Digby of Minterne in Dorsetshire, England, who flowered it for the first time in 1845.

Rhyncholaelia glauca

PRONUNCIATION: rink-oh-LAY-lee-a

AKA: *Brassavola glauca*

ORIGIN: Mexico, Guatemala, Honduras

DESCRIPTION AND QUALITIES: Another fragrant beauty that is easier to grow than its revered cousin, *Rhyncholaelia digbyana*.

INTENSITY OF FRAGRANCE: Strong

WHEN FRAGRANT: Evening

DESCRIPTION OF FRAGRANCE: Rose, lily-of-the-valley, cyclamen, raspberry

FLOWER DESCRIPTION: Pale green flowers with white lips. Flowers about 2½ inches (6.5 cm) wide. Inflorescence 3–6 inches long, with a single flower.

SEASON OF BLOOM: Spring

MATURE PLANT: Compact habit. Leaves grow to about 5 inches (12.5 cm) long.

EASE OF CULTURE: Intermediate

SUITABLE GROWING AREA: Windowsill, lights, greenhouse

LIGHT: Medium

TEMPERATURE: Warm

RECOMMENDED POTTING MEDIUM: Medium-textured epiphytic mix

COMMENT: Originally found by J. Henchman in the 1800s in Mexico.

Rhyncholaelia glauca is a popular species because of its sweet fragrance and showy flower.

Hybrids

Brassocattleya Binosa 'Kirk' AM/AOS

PRONUNCIATION: brass-oh-KAT-lee-a

ORIGIN: *Brassavola nodosa* × *Cattleya bicolor*

FRAGRANT PARENTS: Both parents

DESCRIPTION AND QUALITIES: Binosa is a popular grex because it usually results in very compact, colorful plants that are also fragrant.

INTENSITY OF FRAGRANCE: Light

WHEN FRAGRANT: Evening

DESCRIPTION OF FRAGRANCE: Spicy

FLOWER DESCRIPTION: Bright green sepals and petals, white lips flared and sprinkled with purple spots. Flowers 3 inches (7.5 cm) wide. Inflorescence 4 inches (10 cm) long, with one or two flowers.

SEASON OF BLOOM: Variable

MATURE PLANT: A compact grower, reaching 8–10 inches (20–30 cm) tall.

EASE OF CULTURE: Easy

SUITABLE GROWING AREA: Windowsill, greenhouse

LIGHT: Medium to high

TEMPERATURE: Intermediate to warm

RECOMMENDED POTTING MEDIUM: Medium-textured, well-drained mix

OTHER FRAGRANT BRASSOCATTTLEYAS: *Bc.* Mount Hood—vanilla

Brassocattleya Binosa 'Kirk' AM/AOS combines a sweet scent with striking colors.

Brassolaeliocattleya Formosan Gold

PRONUNCIATION: brass-oh-lay-lee-oh-KAT-lee-a

ORIGIN: *Laeliocattleya* Lorraine Shirai × *Brassolaeliocattleya* Spun Gold

DESCRIPTION AND QUALITIES: An extremely attractive bicolored orchid.

INTENSITY OF FRAGRANCE: Strong

WHEN FRAGRANT: Day

DESCRIPTION OF FRAGRANCE: Vanilla

FLOWER DESCRIPTION: Golden yellow petals and sepals with dark red ruffled lips. Flowers about $4^1/_2$ inches (11 cm) wide. Inflorescence 6 inches (15 cm) tall, with one flower.

SEASON OF BLOOM: Winter

MATURE PLANT: Standard cattleya size.

EASE OF CULTURE: Intermediate

SUITABLE GROWING AREA: Windowsill, greenhouse

LIGHT: Medium to high

TEMPERATURE: Intermediate

RECOMMENDED POTTING MEDIUM: Medium-textured bark or coco chunk mix

The dramatic contrast of the rich red lip against gold petals makes *Brassolaeliocattleya* Formosan Gold stand out.

Brassolaeliocattleya Goldenzelle 'Lemon Chiffon' AM/AOS

PRONUNCIATION: brass-oh-lay-lee-oh-KAT-lee-a

ORIGIN: *Brassolaeliocattleya* Fortune × *Cattleya* Horace

DESCRIPTION AND QUALITIES: The soft yellow flower of this cattleya makes it distinct and in demand.

INTENSITY OF FRAGRANCE: Strong

WHEN FRAGRANT: Day

DESCRIPTION OF FRAGRANCE: Sweet floral

FLOWER DESCRIPTION: Lemon yellow flowers with a splash of deep red on the lips. Flowers 6 inches (15 cm) across. Inflorescence 6 inches (15 cm), bearing one or two flowers.

SEASON OF BLOOM: Winter

MATURE PLANT: Standard cattleya size.

The cultivar name of *Brassolaeliocattleya* Goldenzelle 'Lemon Chiffon' AM/AOS says it all.

EASE OF CULTURE: Intermediate

SUITABLE GROWING AREA: Windowsill, greenhouse

LIGHT: Medium to high

TEMPERATURE: Intermediate

RECOMMENDED POTTING MEDIUM: Medium-textured bark or coco chunk mix

COMMENT: A plant frequently displayed and awarded at orchid shows.

Brassolaeliocattleya Hawaiian Avalanche

PRONUNCIATION: brass-oh-lay-lee-oh-KAT-lee-a

ORIGIN: *Brassolaeliocattleya* Oconee × *Brassolaeliocattleya* George King

FRAGRANT PARENTS: *Brassolaeliocattleya* George King

DESCRIPTION AND QUALITIES: A popular hybrid with a prizewinning parent, *Brassolaeliocattleya* George King.

INTENSITY OF FRAGRANCE: Strong

WHEN FRAGRANT: Day

DESCRIPTION OF FRAGRANCE: Sweet floral, vanilla

FLOWER DESCRIPTION: Apricot pink flowers with golden-orange fringed lips and a purple flare down the center of the lip. Flower 6 inches (15 cm) wide. Inflorescence 6 inches (15 cm) tall, bearing one or two flowers.

SEASON OF BLOOM: Winter

MATURE PLANT: Standard cattleya size.

Brassolaeliocattleya Hawaiian Avalanche shows off a delightful display of tropical color.

EASE OF CULTURE: Intermediate

SUITABLE GROWING AREA: Windowsill, greenhouse

LIGHT: Medium to high

TEMPERATURE: Intermediate

RECOMMENDED POTTING MEDIUM: Medium-textured, well-drained mix

Brassolaeliocattleya Pamela Hetherington 'Coronation' FCC/AOS

PRONUNCIATION: brass-oh-lay-lee-oh-KAT-lee-a

ORIGIN: *Laeliocattleya* Paradisio × *Brassocattleya* Mount Anderson

DESCRIPTION AND QUALITIES: This cattleya hybrid is among the very few to be awarded a First Class Certificate (FCC), the American Orchid Society's highest accolade.

INTENSITY OF FRAGRANCE: Strong

WHEN FRAGRANT: Day

DESCRIPTION OF FRAGRANCE: Sweet floral

FLOWER DESCRIPTION: Lavender-pink flowers with pink ruffled lips and orange-yellow throats. Flowers 6 inches (15 cm) wide. Inflorescence 6 inches (15 cm) tall, bearing one to three flowers.

SEASON OF BLOOM: Winter

MATURE PLANT: Standard cattleya size.

EASE OF CULTURE: Intermediate

SUITABLE GROWING AREA: Windowsill, greenhouse

LIGHT: Medium to high

TEMPERATURE: Intermediate

RECOMMENDED POTTING MEDIUM: Medium-textured bark or coco chunk mix

COMMENTS: Named for a family member of the illustrious orchid breeder, Ernest Hetherington.

OTHER FRAGRANT BRASSO-LAELIOCATTLEYAS: *Blc.* Arthur Bossin 'Rapture'—sweet floral; *Blc.* George King 'Serendipity' AM/AOS—vanilla; *Blc.* Haw Yuan Beauty 'Orchis'—vanilla; *Blc.* Momilani Rainbow—sweet floral; *Blc.* Ports of Paradise 'Emerald Isle' HCC/AOS—citrus; *Blc.* Rio's Green Magic—citrus.

Brassolaeliocattleya Pamela Hetherington 'Coronation' FCC/AOS has a sweet floral scent.

Cattleya Chocolate Drop 'Kodama' AM/AOS

PRONUNCIATION: KAT-lee-a

ORIGIN: *Cattleya guttata × Cattleya aurantiaca*

DESCRIPTION AND QUALITIES: Valued for its many glossy red flowers and
ease of culture.

INTENSITY OF FRAGRANCE: Strong

WHEN FRAGRANT: Day

DESCRIPTION OF FRAGRANCE: Lily-of-the-valley, citrus, rose, lily

FLOWER DESCRIPTION: Glossy, dark red flowers with yellow on the side lobes
of the lip. Flowers $2^{1}/_{2}$ inches (6 cm) wide. Inflorescence 8 inches (20
cm), bearing clusters of up to 20 flowers.

SEASON OF BLOOM: Fall

MATURE PLANT: Standard cattleya size.

EASE OF CULTURE: Easy

SUITABLE GROWING AREA: Windowsill, greenhouse

LIGHT: Medium

TEMPERATURE: Intermediate

RECOMMENDED POTTING MEDIUM: Medium-textured, well-drained mix

COMMENT: Chocolate Drop, a primary hybrid registered in 1965, has been
very popular as a parent.

PLATE 42. *Cattleya* Chocolate Drop 'Kodama' AM/AOS is a fine clone of a very popular
hybrid.

Epicattleya Dora Tinschert 'Springdale' HCC/AOS

PRONUNCIATION: eh-pi-KAT-lee-a

ORIGIN: *Cattleya aurantiaca × Epidendrum selligerum*

DESCRIPTION AND QUALITIES: Two popular parents combine in this cross to produce a fragrant, easy-to-grow hybrid.

INTENSITY OF FRAGRANCE: Strong

WHEN FRAGRANT: Day

DESCRIPTION OF FRAGRANCE: Sweet floral

FLOWER DESCRIPTION: Rusty red-orange flowers with pink-tinged lips. Flowers 3 inches (7.5 cm) wide. Inflorescence 8 inches (20 cm) tall, bearing six or more flowers.

SEASON OF BLOOM: Spring

MATURE PLANT: Reaches 12–18 inches (30–45 cm) tall.

EASE OF CULTURE: Easy

SUITABLE GROWING AREA: Windowsill, greenhouse

LIGHT: Medium

TEMPERATURE: Intermediate

RECOMMENDED POTTING MEDIUM: Medium-textured epiphytic mix

Epicattleya Dora Tinschert 'Springdale' HCC/AOS was one of the sweet-scented favorites in the 2004 New York International Orchid Show fragrance competition.

The color, shape, and heady citrus scent of the flower of *Laeliocattleya* Angel Love owe much to one of the grandparents, *Cattleya walkeriana.*

Laeliocattleya Angel Love

PRONUNCIATION: lay-lee-oh-KAT-lee-a
ORIGIN: *Laeliocattleya* Puppy Love ×
   Laeliocattleya Angelwalker
FRAGRANT PARENTS: *Cattleya walkeriana* (grandparent)
DESCRIPTION AND QUALITIES: This hybrid has the same wonderful fragrance as *Cattleya walkeriana*, but is easier to grow.
INTENSITY OF FRAGRANCE: Strong
WHEN FRAGRANT: Day
DESCRIPTION OF FRAGRANCE: Citrus
FLOWER DESCRIPTION: Pink flowers with frilled lips and golden to yellow throats. Flowers 4 inches (10 cm) across. Inflorescence 3 inches (7.5 cm) tall, bearing one or two flowers.
SEASON OF BLOOM: Variable
MATURE PLANT: Compact hybrid. Gets small habit from *Cattleya walkeriana*.
EASE OF CULTURE: Intermediate
SUITABLE GROWING AREA: Windowsill, lights, greenhouse
LIGHT: Medium
TEMPERATURE: Intermediate
RECOMMENDED POTTING MEDIUM: Medium-textured epiphytic mix

Laeliocattleya Mari's Song 'CTM 217' HCC/AOS

PRONUNCIATION: lay-lee-oh-KAT-lee-a
ORIGIN: *Laeliocattleya* Irene Finney × *Cattleya* Cherry Chip
DESCRIPTION AND QUALITIES: A popular compact, fragrant, splash-petaled cattleya.
INTENSITY OF FRAGRANCE: Strong
WHEN FRAGRANT: Day
DESCRIPTION OF FRAGRANCE: Sweet floral
FLOWER DESCRIPTION: White flowers with bright magenta flares and lips, pink sepals, and yellow throats. Flowers 4½ inches (11 cm) wide. Inflorescence 6 inches (15 cm) tall, bearing two to four flowers.
SEASON OF BLOOM: Variable
MATURE PLANT: Very compact grower, less than 12 inches (30 cm) tall.
EASE OF CULTURE: Easy
SUITABLE GROWING AREA: Windowsill, lights, greenhouse
LIGHT: Medium to high

Laeliocattleya Mari's Song 'CTM 217' HCC/AOS is a favorite among windowsill and light growers because of its compact habit and colorful show. Photo by Bill Norton.

TEMPERATURE: Intermediate
RECOMMENDED POTTING MEDIUM: Cattleya mix
COMMENT: One of the more recent fragrant minicatts.

Potinara **Burana Beauty 'Burana'** HCC/AOS
PRONUNCIATION: pot-tin-AH-rah
ORIGIN: *Potinara* Netrasiri Starbright × *Cattleya* Netrasiri Beauty #4

The citrus fragrance of the compact-growing *Potinara* Burana Beauty 'Burana' HCC/AOS can fill up an entire room.

DESCRIPTION AND QUALITIES: The genus Potinara has parents from four different genera—*Brassavola, Cattleya, Laelia,* and *Sophronitis.*

INTENSITY OF FRAGRANCE: Strong

WHEN FRAGRANT: Day

DESCRIPTION OF FRAGRANCE: Citrus

FLOWER DESCRIPTION: Yellow-green sepals and petals, both with red flares. Flowers 3$^{1}/_{2}$ inches (9-cm) across. Inflorescence 8 inches (20 cm) tall, three to six flowers.

SEASON OF BLOOM: Variable

MATURE PLANT: A compact grower, about 12 inches (30 cm) high.

EASE OF CULTURE: Easy

SUITABLE GROWING AREA: Windowsill, greenhouse, lights

LIGHT: Medium

TEMPERATURE: Intermediate

RECOMMENDED POTTING MEDIUM: Medium-textured cattleya mix

Potinara Twentyfour Carat 'Lea' AM/AOS

PRONUNCIATION: pot-tin-AH-rah

ORIGIN: *Potinara* Lemon Tree × *Brassolaeliocattleya* Yellow Imp

The sunny golden-yellow flowers make *Potinara* Twentyfour Carat 'Lea' AM/AOS stand out.

DESCRIPTION AND QUALITIES: A scented, cheerful variety for a windowsill.

INTENSITY OF FRAGRANCE: Strong

WHEN FRAGRANT: Day

DESCRIPTION OF FRAGRANCE: Vanilla

FLOWER DESCRIPTION: Clear golden-yellow flowers with flared lips. Flowers 4 inches (10 cm) across. Inflorescence 6 inches (15 cm) tall, bearing one or two flowers.

SEASON OF BLOOM: Spring

MATURE PLANT: Slightly smaller than standard cattleya size.

EASE OF CULTURE: Intermediate

SUITABLE GROWING AREA: Windowsill, greenhouse, lights

LIGHT: Medium

TEMPERATURE: Intermediate

RECOMMENDED POTTING MEDIUM: Medium-textured epiphytic mix

Chapter 5

The Dendrobium Tribe

This group of orchids is immense. With more than 1000 species, the dendrobiums are one of the largest groups in the orchid family. They hail from the Old World tropics—China, India, Malaysia, Borneo, New Guinea, New Zealand, and Australia—and are just now starting to receive the attention from orchid growers that they deserve. The following is just a sampling of these impressive orchids.

Species

Bulbophyllum rothschildianum
PRONUNCIATION: bulb-oh-FILL-um
AKA: *Cirrhopetalum rothschildianum*
ORIGIN: India
DESCRIPTION AND QUALITIES: One of the most spectacular *Bulbophyllum* species.
INTENSITY OF FRAGRANCE: Light
WHEN FRAGRANT: Day
DESCRIPTION OF FRAGRANCE: Peach, fruity
FLOWER DESCRIPTION: Rusty red flowers about 1 inch (2.5 cm) wide and up to 7 inches (17.5 cm) long. Inflorescence is an umbel, 10–12 inches (26–30 cm) tall, with five or six flowers.
SEASON OF BLOOM: Summer to fall
MATURE PLANT: Reaches about 12 inches (30 cm) high.
EASE OF CULTURE: Easy
SUITABLE GROWING AREA: Windowsill, lights, greenhouse
LIGHT: Medium
TEMPERATURE: Intermediate to warm

Bulbophyllum rothschildianum 'Red Chimney', awarded as *Cirrhopetalum rothschildianum* 'Red Chimney' FCC/AOS, is considered one of the finest forms of the species.

Dendrobium chrysotoxum shows off bright yellow fragrant flowers with fringed lips.

RECOMMENDED POTTING MEDIUM: Mounted on a slab of tree fern or in a well-drained mix in a shallow container

COMMENT: First described as a *Cirrhopetalum* by James O'Brien in 1895.

OTHER FRAGRANT BULBOPHYLLUMS: *Bulb. ambrosia*—honey, bitter almonds; *Bulb. cocoinum*—coconut; *Bulb. comosum*—hay scented; *Bulb. hamatipes*—musky; *Bulb. laxiflorum*—musky; *Bulb. lobbii*—jasmine, orange blossoms; *Bulb. maximum*—musky; *Bulb. odoratissimum*—pleasant fragrance; *Bulb. suavissimum*—musky.

Dendrobium chrysotoxum

PRONUNCIATION: den-DROH-bee-um

ORIGIN: India, Thailand

DESCRIPTION AND QUALITIES: A brilliant and cheery orchid.

INTENSITY OF FRAGRANCE: Light

WHEN FRAGRANT: Day

DESCRIPTION OF FRAGRANCE: Pineapple, melon, mango

FLOWER DESCRIPTION: Butter yellow flowers with fringed lips and darker orange throats. Flowers 1 inch (2.5 cm) across, short-lived, no more than 10 days. Inflorescence a spike 12 inches (30 cm) long, bearing 6 to 12 or more flowers, depending on the size of the plant.

SEASON OF BLOOM: Spring to summer

MATURE PLANT: A compact, evergreen plant.

EASE OF CULTURE: Intermediate

SUITABLE GROWING AREA: Windowsill, greenhouse

LIGHT: Medium to high

TEMPERATURE: Intermediate

RECOMMENDED POTTING MEDIUM: Well-drained, medium-textured epiphytic mix or mounted
SPECIAL CULTURAL TIP: Keep on the dry side during winter.
COMMENT: First described by John Lindley in 1847.

Dendrobium heterocarpum

PRONUNCIATION: den-DROH-bee-um
AKA: *Dendrobium aureum, Dendrobium rhombeum*
ORIGIN: India to China, Malaysia, Philippines
DESCRIPTION AND QUALITIES: One of the most widely distributed *Dendrobium* species.
INTENSITY OF FRAGRANCE: Strong
WHEN FRAGRANT: Day
DESCRIPTION OF FRAGRANCE: Honeysuckle, primrose
FLOWER DESCRIPTION: Creamy yellow flowers with darker yellow lips streaked with red. Flowers $1^1/_2$–$2^3/_4$ inches (4–7 cm) across. Inflorescence short, 2 inches (5 cm), bearing two to three flowers.
SEASON OF BLOOM: Winter
MATURE PLANT: Erect canes range 8–16 inches (20–50 cm) high.
EASE OF CULTURE: Intermediate
SUITABLE GROWING AREA: Windowsill, greenhouse
LIGHT: Medium to high

Dendrobium heterocarpum is a highly valuable species, ranging from 6 to 50 inches (15–120 cm) in height. Flower color also varies from cream to amber.

TEMPERATURE: Intermediate

RECOMMENDED POTTING MEDIUM: Medium-textured, well-drained epiphytic mix

SPECIAL CULTURAL TIP: Give a dry resting period in the winter and early
spring.

COMMENT: First described by John Lindley in 1830.

Dendrobium jenkinsii

PRONUNCIATION: den-DROH-bee-um

AKA: *Dendrobium lindleyi* var. *jenkinsii*

ORIGIN: India

Dendrobium jenkinsii is a bright, fragrant, and welcomed addition to any
orchid collection.

DESCRIPTION AND QUALITIES: Similar to *Dendrobium lindleyi* but smaller in habit.

INTENSITY OF FRAGRANCE: Mild

WHEN FRAGRANT: Day

DESCRIPTION OF FRAGRANCE: Honey

FLOWER DESCRIPTION: Golden yellow flowers with wide, almost heart-shaped lips. Flowers about 1 inch (2.5 cm) across, lasting 7 to 10 days. Inflorescence about 3 inches (7.5 cm) tall, with flowers in groups of two or three.

SEASON OF BLOOM: Winter to spring

MATURE PLANT: A miniature grower. Pseudobulbs only reach slightly over 1 inch (2.5 cm) tall. The plant can spread to 4 or more inches (10 cm) wide.

EASE OF CULTURE: Intermediate

SUITABLE GROWING AREA: Windowsill, lights, greenhouse

LIGHT: Medium to high

TEMPERATURE: Intermediate

RECOMMENDED POTTING MEDIUM: Mounted on a slab of tree fern or cork, or in a well-drained mix in a pot

SPECIAL CULTURAL TIP: Transplant very infrequently so as not to disturb roots.

COMMENT: Develops as a superb specimen plant. Discovered in 1836 in India by a military man named Jenkins.

Dendrobium kingianum

PRONUNCIATION: den-DROH-bee-um

ORIGIN: Australia

DESCRIPTION AND QUALITIES: One of the easiest Australian orchids to grow. Adapts well to a variety of growing situations.

INTENSITY OF FRAGRANCE: Strong

WHEN FRAGRANT: Day

DESCRIPTION OF FRAGRANCE: Floral, hyacinth, lilac, honey

FLOWER DESCRIPTION: Flowers display a huge range of colors including purple, red, white, and striped. They average about 1–1½ inches (2.5–4 cm) across and last about two weeks. The flowers of some clones or selections are more fragrant than others. Inflorescence up to 8 inches (20 cm) long, bearing two to nine flowers.

SEASON OF BLOOM: Spring

MATURE PLANT: A variable species, from a dwarf growth habit under 6 inches (15 cm) to 20 inches (50 cm). The foliage is attractive and dark green.

EASE OF CULTURE: Easy

SUITABLE GROWING AREA: Windowsill, lights, greenhouse

LIGHT: Medium to high

Dendrobium macrophyllum

PRONUNCIATION: den-DROH-bee-um

AKA: *Dendrobium veitchianum*

ORIGIN: Java to Philippines to Samoa

DESCRIPTION AND QUALITIES: The flowers have an out-of-this-world look that always creates attention.

INTENSITY OF FRAGRANCE: Light

WHEN FRAGRANT: Day

DESCRIPTION OF FRAGRANCE: Sweet floral

FLOWER DESCRIPTION: Variably colored flowers 2 inches (5 cm) across and long-lasting. Inflorescence a spike 6–15 inches (15–40 cm) tall and bearing up to 10 flowers.

SEASON OF BLOOM: Spring to summer

MATURE PLANT: Pseudobulbs up to 24 inches (60 cm) long. Leaves up to 12 inches (30 cm) long.

EASE OF CULTURE: Intermediate

SUITABLE GROWING AREA: Greenhouse

LIGHT: Medium to high

TEMPERATURE: Intermediate

RECOMMENDED POTTING MEDIUM: Medium-textured, well-drained mix

SPECIAL CULTURAL TIP: Keep damp year-round.

COMMENT: First described in 1834 by French botanist Achille Richard.

The exotic coloration, lip markings, and fragrance make *Dendrobium macrophyllum* an Old World orchid that most orchid growers would love to have in their collection.

Hybrids

Dendrobium Chrystaline

PRONUNCIATION: den-DROH-bee-um

ORIGIN: *Dendrobium* Kathryn Banks × *Dendrobium* Bicentennial Blush

DESCRIPTION AND QUALITIES: A hybrid with *Dendrobium kingianum* in its background.

INTENSITY OF FRAGRANCE: Strong

WHEN FRAGRANT: Day

DESCRIPTION OF FRAGRANCE: Hyacinth

FLOWER DESCRIPTION: White flowers with purple markings in the lips. Flowers $1^1/4$ inches (3 cm) across. Inflorescence 10 inches (25 cm) tall, bearing six to eight flowers.

SEASON OF BLOOM: Variable

MATURE PLANT: Compact growing.

EASE OF CULTURE: Easy

SUITABLE GROWING AREA: Windowsill, lights, greenhouse

LIGHT: Medium

TEMPERATURE: Cool to intermediate

RECOMMENDED POTTING MEDIUM: Medium-textured epiphytic mix

The cultivar name describes well the glistening flowers of *Dendrobium* Chrystaline.

Dendrobium Comet King 'Akatsuki' can be depended on for profuse production of brightly colored, perfumed blossoms.

Dendrobium Comet King 'Akatsuki'

PRONUNCIATION: den-DROH-bee-um
ORIGIN: *Dendrobium* New Comet ×
   Dendrobium Wave King
DESCRIPTION AND QUALITIES: One of
   more than 100 nobile-type hybrids
   that are popular because of their
   many flowers, bright colors, and
   ease of flowering.
INTENSITY OF FRAGRANCE: Light
WHEN FRAGRANT: Day
DESCRIPTION OF FRAGRANCE: Sweet
   floral
FLOWER DESCRIPTION: Purple flowers
   with golden centers, flowers $2^1/_2$
   inches (6 cm) across and long-last-
   ing. Inflorescence short and bearing
   flowers in such abundance that they
   present a "bouquet" effect.
SEASON OF BLOOM: Variable
MATURE PLANT: Reaches 12–18 inches
   (30–45 cm) tall.
EASE OF CULTURE: Easy
SUITABLE GROWING AREA: Windowsill,
   greenhouse
LIGHT: Medium to high
TEMPERATURE: Intermediate
RECOMMENDED POTTING MEDIUM: Medium-textured epiphytic mix
SPECIAL CULTURAL TIP: Keep cool (45–50°F/7–10°C) and dry in the fall or
   winter to set buds for spring flowering.
COMMENT: This dendrobium does not lose it leaves until the second year.

Dendrobium Jesmond Gem

PRONUNCIATION: den-DROH-bee-um
ORIGIN: *Dendrobium* Yondi × *Dendrobium speciosum*
FRAGRANT PARENTS: *Dendrobium speciosum*
DESCRIPTION AND QUALITIES: A tough Australian hybrid that can tolerate
   temperatures close to freezing with little damage.
INTENSITY OF FRAGRANCE: Strong
WHEN FRAGRANT: Day
DESCRIPTION OF FRAGRANCE: Sweet floral

The pristine white, sweet-smelling flowers of *Dendrobium* Jesmond Gem make this hybrid a standout.

FLOWER DESCRIPTION: White flowers with purple specks on lips and yellow stripes down center of the lips. Flowers 2 inches (5 cm) across. Inflorescence 6–8 inches (15–20 cm) tall, bearing 8 to 10 flowers.

SEASON OF BLOOM: Winter to spring

MATURE PLANT: Reaches about 18 inches (45 cm) tall.

EASE OF CULTURE: Intermediate

SUITABLE GROWING AREA: Windowsill, greenhouse

LIGHT: Medium to high

TEMPERATURE: Cool to intermediate

RECOMMENDED POTTING MEDIUM: Medium-textured bark mix

SPECIAL CULTURAL TIP: Cool off in the fall to 40 to 49°F (4–9°C) to set buds.

Dendrobium Light River

PRONUNCIATION: den-DROH-bee-um
ORIGIN: *Dendrobium* Red River × *Dendrobium speciosum*
FRAGRANT PARENTS: *Dendrobium speciosum*

Australian hybrids like *Dendrobium* Light River are quickly gaining popularity because of their low temperature requirements, long blooming period, and fragrance.

DESCRIPTION AND QUALITIES: Another Australian hybrid that is stunning and dependable.

INTENSITY OF FRAGRANCE: Strong

WHEN FRAGRANT: Day

DESCRIPTION OF FRAGRANCE: Sweet floral

FLOWER DESCRIPTION: Creamy flowers with purple markings. Lip brightly marked in purple with yellow in the center. Flowers 2 inches (5 cm) across. Inflorescence 6–8 inches (15–20 cm) tall, bearing 8 to 10 flowers.

SEASON OF BLOOM: Winter

MATURE PLANT: Reaches about 18 inches (45 cm) tall.

EASE OF CULTURE: Intermediate

SUITABLE GROWING AREA: Windowsill, greenhouse

LIGHT: Medium to high

TEMPERATURE: Cool to intermediate

RECOMMENDED POTTING MEDIUM: Medium-textured cattleya mix

SPECIAL CULTURAL TIP: Cool off in the fall to 40 to 49°F (4–9°C) to set buds.

Chapter 6

The Oncidium Alliance

There is something particularly joyful about the members of the Oncidium Alliance. They sport some of the brightest and wildest color combinations in the orchid family. Many of them are easy to grow and have a broad range of pleasing fragrances.

Species

Brassia longissima
PRONUNCIATION: BRASS-ee-ah
AKA: *Brassia lawrenceana*
ORIGIN: Costa Rica, Panama, Peru
DESCRIPTION AND QUALITIES: The spider-like flower makes a dramatic statement.
INTENSITY OF FRAGRANCE: Light
WHEN FRAGRANT: Day
DESCRIPTION OF FRAGRANCE: Light, sweet candy
FLOWER DESCRIPTION: Large, spidery flowers open greenish and turn orange over several days. Petals, sepals, and lip are spotted maroon. Flowers 7–8 inches (18–20 cm) long. Inflorescence to 18 inches (45 cm) tall, bearing six to eight flowers.
SEASON OF BLOOM: Summer to fall
MATURE PLANT: Reaches about 30 inches (75 cm) tall.
EASE OF CULTURE: Easy
SUITABLE GROWING AREA: Windowsill, greenhouse
LIGHT: Medium to high
TEMPERATURE: Warm
RECOMMENDED POTTING MEDIUM: Medium-textured, well drained mix

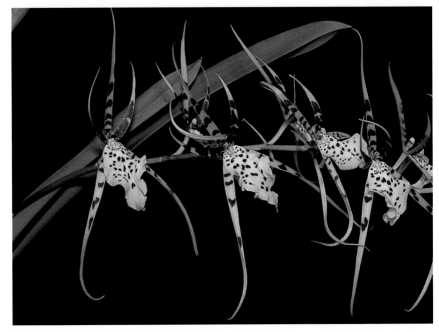

The spidery flowers of *Brassia longissima* 'Pumpkin Patch' line up to parade themselves.

COMMENT: First flowered in cultivation by W. Butler in England in 1868.
OTHER FRAGRANT BRASSIAS: *Brs. gireoudiana*—musky; *Brs. ochroleuca*—spicy, spiced apple pie; *Brs. verrucosa*—musky.

Miltonia spectabilis

PRONUNCIATION: mil-TONE-ee-ah
AKA: *Macrochilus fryanus*
ORIGIN: Brazil
DESCRIPTION AND QUALITIES: This is the largest flowering species in this genus.
INTENSITY OF FRAGRANCE: Strong
WHEN FRAGRANT: Day
DESCRIPTION OF FRAGRANCE: Rose, spicy
FLOWER DESCRIPTION: White flowers tinged pink with rose-pink lips and purple columns. Flowers 4 inches (10 cm) wide. Inflorescence 8 inches (20 cm) tall, bearing a single flower.
SEASON OF BLOOM: Summer to fall
MATURE PLANT: Reaches 10 inches (25 cm) tall.
EASE OF CULTURE: Intermediate
SUITABLE GROWING AREA: Windowsill, greenhouse, lights
LIGHT: Medium

TEMPERATURE: Intermediate

RECOMMENDED POTTING MEDIUM:
Fine-textured, well-drained mix

SPECIAL CULTURAL TIP: As is true for
other miltonias, keep the growing
medium damp.

COMMENT: The species was first
described in 1839 by John Lindley
from a specimen collected in
Brazil by Hugh Weddell.

OTHER FRAGRANT MILTONIAS: *Milt.
regnellii*—oranges, coriander;
Milt. schroederiana—spice floral,
carnation.

Miltonia spectabilis var. moreliana

PRONUNCIATION: mil-TONE-ee-ah

ORIGIN: Brazil

DESCRIPTION AND QUALITIES: Has
long-lasting flowers.

INTENSITY OF FRAGRANCE: Strong

WHEN FRAGRANT: Day

DESCRIPTION OF FRAGRANCE: Rose,
spicy

FLOWER DESCRIPTION: Dark plum
red petals and sepals contrast
with a large bright rose-pink lip
with darker veins. Flowers 4
inches (10 cm) wide. Inflorescence 8 inches (20 cm) tall, with
a single flower.

SEASON OF BLOOM: Summer to fall

MATURE PLANT: Reaches 10 inches
(25 cm) high.

EASE OF CULTURE: Intermediate

SUITABLE GROWING AREA: Windowsill, greenhouse, lights

LIGHT: Medium

TEMPERATURE: Intermediate

RECOMMENDED POTTING MEDIUM:
Fine-textured, well-drained mix

Miltonia spectabilis presents an elegant
picture.

Miltonia spectabilis var. *moreliana* is a
spectacular variant of the species.

Oncidium cheirophorum is a bright and cheery dwarf, fragrant orchid.

DESCRIPTION OF FRAGRANCE: Citrus, lemon

FLOWER DESCRIPTION: Bright yellow flowers on a branched arching spray. Many flowers, 1/2 inch (1.3 cm) wide. Inflorescence to 12 inches (30 cm) long.

SEASON OF BLOOM: Winter to spring

MATURE PLANT: Reaches only 3 inches (7.5 cm) high.

EASE OF CULTURE: Easy

SUITABLE GROWING AREA: Windowsill, lights, greenhouse

LIGHT: Medium

TEMPERATURE: Intermediate

RECOMMENDED POTTING MEDIUM: Fine- to medium-textured orchid mix

COMMENT: Very easy to grow and bloom. Described by H. G. Reichenbach in 1852 and discovered by the famous Lithuanian plant collector, Józef Ritter von Rawicz Warscewicz.

Oncidium maculatum

PRONUNCIATION: on-SID-ee-um

ORIGIN: Mexico

DESCRIPTION AND QUALITIES: An attractive and easy-to-grow species.

INTENSITY OF FRAGRANCE: Strong

WHEN FRAGRANT: Day

DESCRIPTION OF FRAGRANCE: Honey

FLOWER DESCRIPTION: Yellow flowers with mahogany spots. Flowers 3 inches (8 cm) wide. Inflorescence an arching spike 20 inches (50 cm) long, with many flowers.

SEASON OF BLOOM: Spring

MATURE PLANT: Medium-large, dark green leaves.

EASE OF CULTURE: Easy

SUITABLE GROWING AREA: Windowsill, greenhouse

Oncidium maculatum has well-marked honey-scented flowers.

LIGHT: Medium
TEMPERATURE: Intermediate
RECOMMENDED POTTING MEDIUM: Very well drained potting material in a pot or basket
SPECIAL CULTURAL TIP: Provide a dry resting period in winter.

Oncidium ornithorhynchum

PRONUNCIATION: on-SID-ee-um
ORIGIN: Mexico, Guatemala, El Salvador, Costa Rica
COMMON NAME: Vanilla-scented dancing lady, lavender and old lace
DESCRIPTION AND QUALITIES: 'Lilac Blossom' is a select form highly recommended to beginning growers because of its ease of culture, dependable blooming, and sweet fragrance.
INTENSITY OF FRAGRANCE: Strong
WHEN FRAGRANT: Day
DESCRIPTION OF FRAGRANCE: Vanilla, "like a fresh morning," baby powder, grape, spicy, cinnamon, cocoa, sweet candy

FLOWER DESCRIPTION: Lavender-pink flowers produced by the hundreds on a mature plant. Flowers about 1 inch (2.5 cm) across. Inflorescence 24 inches (60 cm) long, with many flowers.

SEASON OF BLOOM: Spring to summer

MATURE PLANT: Reaches 6–8 inches (15–20 cm) high.

EASE OF CULTURE: Easy

Oncidium ornithorhynchum 'Lilac Blossom' comes from Ha'iku Maui Orchids in Hawaii. PHOTO BY MARC HERZOG.

SUITABLE GROWING AREA: Windowsill, lights, greenhouse
LIGHT: Medium
TEMPERATURE: Intermediate
RECOMMENDED POTTING MEDIUM: Fine- to medium-textured orchid mix
COMMENT: First described by German botanist and explorer Alexander von
Humboldt in 1815.

Sigmatostalix radicans

PRONUNCIATION: sig-mat-oh-STAY-licks
ORIGIN: Brazil
DESCRIPTION AND QUALITIES: A delicate-looking but easy-to-grow, sweet-
scented miniature.
INTENSITY OF FRAGRANCE: Light
WHEN FRAGRANT: Day
DESCRIPTION OF FRAGRANCE: Honey
FLOWER DESCRIPTION: Small white flowers with greenish sepals and petals,
a brown column, and white lip. Flowers $3/4$ inch (1 cm) wide. Inflores-
cence 6–8 inches (15–20 cm) tall, bearing many flowers.
SEASON OF BLOOM: Fall
MATURE PLANT: Thin grassy foliage about 6 inches (15 cm) long.
EASE OF CULTURE: Easy

Sigmatostalix radicans 'HMO's Petite Prince', a dainty, charming miniature with grass-
like foliage and a honey scent, comes from Ha'iku Maui Orchids in Hawaii. PHOTO BY
MARC HERZOG.

Suitable growing area: Windowsill, lights, greenhouse
Light: Medium
Temperature: Intermediate
Recommended potting medium: Fine-textured mix
Comment: The genus comprises about 20 species in the American tropics.

Trichopilia suavis

Pronunciation: trik-oh-PILL-ee-ah
Aka: *Trichopilia kienastiana*
Origin: Costa Rica, Panama, Colombia
Description and qualities: The flowers are borne at the bottom of the plant.
Intensity of fragrance: Strong
When fragrant: Day
Description of fragrance: Floral; intoxicating
Flower description: Flowers usually white spotted with red. The lip is tubular and has pink and orange spots. Flowers 4 inches (10 cm) wide. Inflorescence pendant, 4 inches (10 cm) long, bearing two to five flowers.

Trichopilia suavis is considered one of the most attractive species in the genus.

Season of bloom: Spring
Mature plant: Oblong pseudobulbs with leaves about 16 inches (40 cm) long.
Ease of culture: Easy
Suitable growing area: Windowsill, light, greenhouse
Light: Medium
Temperature: Intermediate
Recommended potting medium: Medium-textured, well-drained mix
Special cultural tip: Frequently grown in baskets.
Comment: Discovered by Józef Ritter von Rawicz Warscewicz in Costa Rica in 1848.
Other fragrant trichopilias: *Trpla. fragrans*—narcissus

Hybrids

Beallara Marfitch 'Howard's Dream' AM/AOS

PRONUNCIATION: bee-al-ARE-ah
ORIGIN: *Miltassia* Charles M. Fitch ×
Odontoglossum Fremar
DESCRIPTION AND QUALITIES: This
complex hybrid has parents from
four different genera—*Brassia,
Cochlioda, Miltonia,* and *Odonto-
glossum.*
INTENSITY OF FRAGRANCE: Light
WHEN FRAGRANT: Day
DESCRIPTION OF FRAGRANCE: Rose
FLOWER DESCRIPTION: Star-shaped
flowers burgundy, magenta, and
white, 4–5 inches (10–13 cm) across,
and lasting a few months. Inflores-
cence 24–36 inches (60–90 cm) long,
bearing up to 20 or more flowers.
Can flower twice a year.
SEASON OF BLOOM: Variable
MATURE PLANT: Reaches 18–24 inches
(45–60 cm) tall.
EASE OF CULTURE: Easy
SUITABLE GROWING AREA: Windowsill,
greenhouse
LIGHT: Medium
TEMPERATURE: Intermediate
RECOMMENDED POTTING MEDIUM:
Medium-textured mix with coco
chunks

The color combination of *Beallara* Marfitch
'Howard's Dream' AM/AOS sparkles.

Miltoniopsis Bert Field

PRONUNCIATION: mil-tone-ee-OP-sis
ORIGIN: *Miltoniopsis* Mulatto Queen ×
Miltoniopsis Woodlands
DESCRIPTION AND QUALITIES: A gor-
geous orchid with pansy-shaped
flowers.

Miltoniopsis Bert Field has pure red velvet-
textured flowers.

INTENSITY OF FRAGRANCE: Light

WHEN FRAGRANT: Day

DESCRIPTION OF FRAGRANCE: Light floral

FLOWER DESCRIPTION: Large, variable flowers that may be solid red or have waterfall patterns in the lips. Flowers 3 inches (7.5 cm) wide. Inflorescence 12 inches (30 cm) tall, bearing three to five flowers.

SEASON OF BLOOM: Spring

MATURE PLANT: Reaches 12–16 inches (30–40 cm) tall.

EASE OF CULTURE: Intermediate

SUITABLE GROWING AREA: Windowsill, greenhouse, lights

LIGHT: Low to medium

TEMPERATURE: Cool to intermediate

RECOMMENDED POTTING MEDIUM: Fine-textured, well-drained mix

SPECIAL CULTURAL TIP: Keep the growing medium damp to avoid pleating of the foliage.

Miltoniopsis **Hajime Ono**

PRONUNCIATION: mil-tone-ee-OP-sis

Miltoniopsis Hajime Ono is a spectacular grex, the result of modern breeding efforts to make the waterfall pattern in the lip more prominent.

ORIGIN: *Miltoniopsis* Martin Orenstein × *Miltoniopsis* Pearl Ono

DESCRIPTION AND QUALITIES: The huge flowers are a testament to the progress made by today's orchid breeders.

INTENSITY OF FRAGRANCE: Mild

WHEN FRAGRANT: Day

DESCRIPTION OF FRAGRANCE: Light rose

FLOWER DESCRIPTION: Dark red velvety flowers with a lip fantastically marked with a waterfall pattern. Flowers $3^{1}/_{2}$ inches (9 cm) wide. Inflorescence 12 inches (30 cm) tall, bearing four to six flowers.

SEASON OF BLOOM: Spring

MATURE PLANT: Reaches 12–14 inches (30–35 cm) high.

EASE OF CULTURE: Intermediate

SUITABLE GROWING AREA: Windowsill, greenhouse, lights

LIGHT: Low to medium

TEMPERATURE: Cool to intermediate
RECOMMENDED POTTING MEDIUM: Fine-textured mix
COMMENT: This glorious hybrid was named after the noted Hawaiian miltoniopsis breeder, Hajime Ono.

Odontioda Vesta 'Charm'

PRONUNCIATION: oh-don-TEA-oh-da
ORIGIN: *Odontioda* Charlesworthii × *Odontoglossum* Prince Albert
DESCRIPTION AND QUALITIES: A compact orchid that is perfectly suited for windowsill or under lights culture.
INTENSITY OF FRAGRANCE: Light
WHEN FRAGRANT: Day
DESCRIPTION OF FRAGRANCE: Citrus
FLOWER DESCRIPTION: White flowers with distinct purple and red markings on petals and sepals and with yellow on the throat. Flowers $2^{1}/_{2}$ inches (6.5-cm) in diameter.
SEASON OF BLOOM: Variable
MATURE PLANT: Compact growing, 6–8 inches (15–20 cm) tall. Foliage light green, about 1 inch (2.5 cm) wide.
EASE OF CULTURE: Easy
SUITABLE GROWING AREA: Windowsill, lights, greenhouse
LIGHT: Low to medium
TEMPERATURE: Intermediate
RECOMMENDED POTTING MEDIUM: Fine-textured epiphytic mix

Odontioda Vesta 'Charm' is a charming plant with a sweet citrus scent.

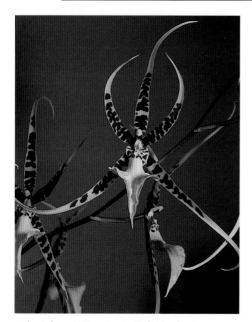

Odontobrassia Fangtastic Bob Henley is a spidery, dramatic beauty.

Oncidium Issaku Nagata 'Volcano Queen' HCC/AOS displays a spectacular spire of blooms on a long spike.

Odontobrassia Fangtastic Bob Henley

PRONUNCIATION: oh-don-toh-BRASS-ee-ah

ORIGIN: *Brassia* Rex × *Odontobrassia* Kenneth Bivin

FRAGRANT PARENTS: *Brassia longissima*

DESCRIPTION AND QUALITIES: *Odontobrassia* is a complex hybrid consisting of *Brassia gireoudiana*, *Brassia longissima*, *Brassia verrucosa* and *Odontoglossum cariniferum*.

INTENSITY OF FRAGRANCE: Light

WHEN FRAGRANT: Day

DESCRIPTION OF FRAGRANCE: Floral

FLOWER DESCRIPTION: Spidery yellow flowers with maroon markings and yellow lip. Flowers 4–5 inches (10–13 cm) across. Inflorescence an arching spike, 24–36 inches (60–90 cm) tall, with many flowers.

SEASON OF BLOOM: Variable

MATURE PLANT: Reaches 18 inches (45 cm) tall.

EASE OF CULTURE: Intermediate

SUITABLE GROWING AREA: Windowsill, greenhouse

LIGHT: Medium

TEMPERATURE: Intermediate

RECOMMENDED POTTING MEDIUM: Fine- to medium-textured mix

Oncidium Issaku Nagata 'Volcano Queen' HCC/AOS

PRONUNCIATION: mil-tone-ID-ee-um

ORIGIN: *Oncidium leucochilum* × *Oncidium warscewiczii*

DESCRIPTION AND QUALITIES: A heavy flowerer that is undemanding in its culture.

INTENSITY OF FRAGRANCE: Light

WHEN FRAGRANT: Day

DESCRIPTION OF FRAGRANCE: Light floral
FLOWER DESCRIPTION: Yellow petals and sepals overlaid with mahogany. The flared lip is white at the bottom and red-purple at the top. Flowers 1 1/2 inches (4-cm) across. Inflorescence a tall multibranched spike, bearing many flowers.
SEASON OF BLOOM: Variable
MATURE PLANT: Foliage 18–24 inches (45-60 cm) long.
EASE OF CULTURE: Easy
SUITABLE GROWING AREA: Windowsill, greenhouse
LIGHT: Medium
TEMPERATURE: Intermediate
RECOMMENDED POTTING MEDIUM: Medium-textured orchid mix for mature plants
COMMENT: An easy-to-grow orchid.

Oncidium Sharry Baby 'Misaki'
PRONUNCIATION: on-SID-ee-um
ORIGIN: *Oncidium* Jamie Sutton × *Oncidium* Honolulu
DESCRIPTION AND QUALITIES: Sharry Baby is a very popular grex.
INTENSITY OF FRAGRANCE: Strong
WHEN FRAGRANT: Day
DESCRIPTION OF FRAGRANCE: Chocolate, vanilla
FLOWER DESCRIPTION: Yellow flowers overlaid with mahogany. Flared white lip has purple markings in center. Flowers 1/2 inch (1.5 cm) wide. Inflorescence a spike, bearing many flowers. Frequently blooms twice a year
SEASON OF BLOOM: Variable
MATURE PLANT: Very fast growing to more than 30 inches tall (75 cm).
EASE OF CULTURE: Easy
SUITABLE GROWING AREA: Windowsill, greenhouse
LIGHT: Medium
TEMPERATURE: Intermediate
RECOMMENDED POTTING MEDIUM: Medium-textured orchid mix
COMMENT: Very easy to grow and bloom. Frequently flowers around Christmas time.

'Misaki' is one of the many select forms of *Oncidium* Sharry Baby.

A sweetly scented miniature plant, *Oncidium* Tsiku Marguerite is an ideal beginner's orchid.

Oncidium Tsiku Marguerite

PRONUNCIATION: on-SID-ee-um

ORIGIN: *Oncidium ornithorhynchum* × *Oncidium* Twinkle

FRAGRANT PARENTS: Both parents

DESCRIPTION AND QUALITIES: A very popular hybrid because of its frequent blooming and ease of culture.

INTENSITY OF FRAGRANCE: Light

WHEN FRAGRANT: Day

DESCRIPTION OF FRAGRANCE: Sweet, soapy

FLOWER DESCRIPTION: Densely branched sprays of $^3/_4$-inch (2-cm) cream to pink flowers with gold lips. Inflorescence 12 inches (30 cm) tall.

SEASON OF BLOOM: Variable

MATURE PLANT: Miniature habit with leaves about 6 inches (15 cm) long.

EASE OF CULTURE: Easy

SUITABLE GROWING AREA: Windowsill, lights, greenhouse

LIGHT: Medium

TEMPERATURE: Intermediate to warm

RECOMMENDED POTTING MEDIUM: Fine-textured mix

COMMENT: One of several crosses using *Oncidium ornithorhynchum* for its dwarf habit and fragrance.

Oncidium Twinkle 'Red Fantasy'

PRONUNCIATION: on-SID-ee-um

ORIGIN: *Oncidium cheirophorum* × *Oncidium ornithorhynchum*

FRAGRANT PARENTS: Both parents

DESCRIPTION AND QUALITIES: Highly recommended as a beginner's orchid because it is so easy to grow and bloom.

INTENSITY OF FRAGRANCE: Strong

WHEN FRAGRANT: Day

DESCRIPTION OF FRAGRANCE: Sweet

FLOWER DESCRIPTION: Rose-colored flowers with darker lips. Flowers 1 inch (2.5 cm) wide. Inflorescence 12 inches (30 cm) tall, with a profusion of flowers. The grex produces many color forms.

SEASON OF BLOOM: Variable

MATURE PLANT: Dwarf, to 6 to 8 inches (15–20 cm) tall.

EASE OF CULTURE: Easy

SUITABLE GROWING AREA: Windowsill, greenhouse, lights

LIGHT: Medium

TEMPERATURE: Intermediate to warm

Combining two outstanding dwarf species resulted in this winning hybrid, *Oncidium* Twinkle 'Red Fantasy'.

RECOMMENDED POTTING MEDIUM: Fine-textured mix

COMMENT: The original Twinkle was registered by famous Hawaiian orchid hybridizer Goodale Moir in 1958.

OTHER FRAGRANT ONCIDIUMS: *Onc.* Twinkle 'Fragrance Fantasy'—sweet.

Trichocentrum Nathakhun

PRONUNCIATION: trik-oh-CEN-trum

ORIGIN: *Trichocentrum lanceanum* × *Trichocentrum* Maui Gold

FRAGRANT PARENTS: *Trichocentrum lanceanum*

DESCRIPTION AND QUALITIES: Called a mule-eared orchid because of the shape of its leaves.

INTENSITY OF FRAGRANCE: Strong

WHEN FRAGRANT: Day

DESCRIPTION OF FRAGRANCE: Honey

FLOWER DESCRIPTION: Flat, long-lasting flowers of contrasting brown and yellow with yellow lip. Flowers $2^{1}/_{2}$ inches (6 cm) in diameter. Inflorescence bears 12 or more flowers.

SEASON OF BLOOM: Spring to summer

MATURE PLANT: Mule ear foliage about 12 inches (30 cm) or more.

EASE OF CULTURE: Intermediate

SUITABLE GROWING AREA: Windowsill, greenhouse

LIGHT: Medium to high

TEMPERATURE: Intermediate to warm

RECOMMENDED POTTING MEDIUM: Medium-textured bark or coco chunk mix

Trichocentrum Nathakhun inherited the striking color combination and honey fragrance from its *Trichocentrum lanceanum* parent.

Chapter 7

The Vanda/Phalaenopsis Alliance

Vandas are probably best known by orchid growers in the American South, particularly, Florida, since the plants thrive in this bright, hot climate, while phalaenopsis are undoubtedly the most widely grown orchid in the world. Neither genera is known for fragrance, but individuals within each genus are sweet scented. Other orchid species and hybrids of this large alliance also contain a good number of fragrant members.

Species

Since all of the orchids in this alliance grow vertically, they can get very tall. So, for these orchids, I have given their approximate spread and height of plants after a few years of mature growth.

Aerangis citrata
PRONUNCIATION: ay-er-RANG-giss
AKA: *Angraecum citratum*
ORIGIN: Africa
DESCRIPTION AND QUALITIES: An easy, choice, and adaptable plant that thrives in lower light conditions and is a very compact grower. It blooms several times a year.
INTENSITY OF FRAGRANCE: Strong
WHEN FRAGRANT: Evening
DESCRIPTION OF FRAGRANCE: Lemon
FLOWER DESCRIPTION: Small, white flowers with long spurs. Inflorescence a spike 6–10 inches (15–25 cm) long, with up to 15 or more flowers.
SEASON OF BLOOM: Spring
MATURE PLANT: Dwarf
EASE OF CULTURE: Easy

Suitable growing area: Windowsill, lights, greenhouse

Light: Medium

Temperature: Intermediate to warm

Recommended potting medium: Fine-textured, well-drained mix

Special cultural tip: Keep in small pots, 3 inches (7.5 cm) in diameter on average, 4 inches (10 cm) maximum. Does best with good air circulation.

Comment: Placed in the genus *Aerangis* in 1822.

Once established, *Aerangis citrata* is an easy orchid to grow. It produces a flurry of flowers with a lemon scent.

OTHER FRAGRANT AERANGIS: *Aergs. appendiculata*—gardenia; *Aergs. articulata*—jasmine; *Aergs. biloba*—gardenia, lily; *Aergs. brachycarpa*—vanilla, jasmine; *Aergs. confusa*—tuberose, gardenia; *Aergs. fastuosa*—tuberose, lily; *Aergs. kirkii*—tuberose, gardenia; *Aergs. kotschyana*—gardenia; *Aergs. modesta*—minty spice; *Aergs. mooreana*—jasmine; *Aergs. mystacidii*—lily of the valley; *Aergs. somalensis*—gardenia.

Aerides fieldingii

PRONUNCIATION: ay-AIR-ee-deez
AKA: *Aerides rosea, Aerides williamsii*
ORIGIN: India
FRAGRANT OFFSPRING: *Aerides* Dominyanum (*Aer. affine* × *Aer. fieldingii*); *Aerides* Dottie's Delight (*Aer. crassifolia* × *Aer. fieldingii*)
DESCRIPTION AND QUALITIES: A specimen plant of this species puts on quite a show.
INTENSITY OF FRAGRANCE: Strong
WHEN FRAGRANT: Day
DESCRIPTION OF FRAGRANCE: Lily-of-the-valley, cyclamen
FLOWER DESCRIPTION: Pink flowers, sometimes spotted. Flowers ³⁄₄ inch (2 cm) wide. Inflorescence a long raceme, 12 inches (60 cm), with up to 30 flowers.
SEASON OF BLOOM: Summer
MATURE PLANT: Leaves 8 inches (25 cm) long.
EASE OF CULTURE: Intermediate
SUITABLE GROWING AREA: Windowsill, greenhouse
LIGHT: Medium
TEMPERATURE: Intermediate to warm
RECOMMENDED POTTING MEDIUM: Medium-textured, very well drained mix
SPECIAL CULTURAL TIP: Keep dry during cooler winters.
COMMENT: First cultivated by Thomas Lobb, plant collector for the famous English orchid firm, Veitch & Sons.

The genus *Aerides* comprises many species that are sweetly scented including this one, *Aerides fieldingii*.

OTHER FRAGRANT AERIDES: *Aer. crassifolia*—aromatic floral; *Aer. falcata* var. *houlletiana*—citrus, fruity; *Aer. falcata*—citrus, fruity; *Aer. lawrenceae*—lemon-spice, honey, anise; *Aer. lawrenceae* var. *sanderiana*—lemon-spice; *Aer. odorata*—spicy; ribbon candy, cloves, lilac; *Aer. quinquevulnera*—cinnamon.

Angraecum leonis

PRONUNCIATION: an-GRYE-kum
AKA: *Aeranthes leonis*
ORIGIN: Madagascar, Comoro Islands
FRAGRANT OFFSPRING: *Angraecum* Hillerman's Last (*Angcm. leonis* × *Angc. superbum*)
DESCRIPTION AND QUALITIES: The species has two different forms: the Madagascan form is smaller vegetatively than the Comoro Island form.
INTENSITY OF FRAGRANCE: Strong
WHEN FRAGRANT: Evening
DESCRIPTION OF FRAGRANCE: Jasmine
FLOWER DESCRIPTION: White flowers $1\frac{1}{2}$ inches (3 cm) wide. Inflorescence a spike, 3–5 inches (7.5–13 cm), with three to five flowers.
SEASON OF BLOOM: Winter to spring

For those who adore the jasmine scent of most angraecums but have limited space, the compact *Angraecum leonis* is the answer.

MATURE PLANT: Reaches 6–10 inches (15–25 cm) tall. Handsome foliage.
EASE OF CULTURE: Easy
SUITABLE GROWING AREA: Windowsill, lights, greenhouse
LIGHT: Medium
TEMPERATURE: Intermediate to warm
RECOMMENDED POTTING MEDIUM: Mounted on a slab or potted in a loose epiphytic mix
COMMENT: A popular species because of its compact habit and relatively large flower. Named by Veitch in 1894.

Angraecum sesquipedale

PRONUNCIATION: an-GRYE-kum
ORIGIN: Madagascar
COMMON NAME: Star of Bethlehem, king of angraecums
FRAGRANT OFFSPRING: *Angraecum* Appalachian Star (*Angcm. sesqui-*

pedale × *Angcm. praestans*); *Angraecum* Dianne's Darling (*Angcm. sesquipedale* × *Angcm.* Alabaster)

DESCRIPTION AND QUALITIES: The largest and showiest of the angraecums.

INTENSITY OF FRAGRANCE: Strong

WHEN FRAGRANT: Evening

DESCRIPTION OF FRAGRANCE: Jasmine

FLOWER DESCRIPTION: Huge waxy white blossoms with a spur up to 15 inches (60 cm) long. Flowers are the largest in the genus, up to 4$^{1}/_{2}$ inches (11 cm) across. Inflorescence 12 inches (30 cm) long, bearing two to four flowers.

SEASON OF BLOOM: Winter

MATURE PLANT: Reaches 24 inches (60 cm) or more high and wide.

EASE OF CULTURE: Intermediate

SUITABLE GROWING AREA: Greenhouse

LIGHT: Medium to high

TEMPERATURE: Warm

RECOMMENDED POTTING MEDIUM: Medium- to coarse-textured fir bark mix

SPECIAL CULTURAL TIP: Do not re-pot younger plants.

COMMENT: This species was made famous by Charles Darwin who postulated the existence of a night-flying moth with an 11-inch (28-cm) proboscis to be able to harvest the nectar located at the end of this flower's long spur. Thirty-five years after Darwin's death, he was proven right when a hawk moth with this proboscis length was found to pollinate this orchid.

OTHER FRAGRANT ANGRAECUMS: *Angcm. aporoides*—gardenia; *Angcm. birrinense*—orange blossom; *Angcm. boisserianum*—jasmine; *Angcm. bosseri*—spicy floral; *Angcm. compactum*—spicy, citrusy; *Angcm. didieri*—sweet, spicy; *Angcm. distichum*—jasmine; *Angcm. eburneum*—gardenia; *Angcm. eichlerianum*—jasmine, lily; *Angcm. germinyanum*—jasmine; *Angcm.* Lemforde White Beauty—jasmine; *Angcm.* Longiscott 'Lea'—jasmine; *Angcm. magdalenae*—jasmine; *Angcm.* Veitchii—jasmine; *Angcm.* White Emblem—jasmine.

Angraecum sesquipedale can grow into a spectacular specimen but requires plenty of room in a bright greenhouse.

Neofinetia falcata

PRONUNCIATION: nee-oh-fin-EE-tha

AKA: *Angraecum falcatum*

ORIGIN: Japan

COMMON NAME: Fu-ran, Japanese wind orchid

FRAGRANT OFFSPRING: *Ascofinetia* Cherry Blossom (*Neofinetia falcata* × *Ascocentrum ampullaceum*); *Darwinara* Charm (*Neofinetia falcata* × *Vascostylis* Tham Yuen Hae)

DESCRIPTION AND QUALITIES: These small plants are easy to bloom in a bright windowsill. Has produced many intergeneric vandaceous hybrids noted for compact growth habit and fragrance.

INTENSITY OF FRAGRANCE: Strong

WHEN FRAGRANT: Day

DESCRIPTION OF FRAGRANCE: Jasmine, vanilla

For all fragrant plant lovers, the diminutive *Neofinetia falcata* is a must.

FLOWER DESCRIPTION: Elegant, snow-white waxy flowers about 1 inch (2.5 cm) wide with a 2-inch (5-cm) spur. Inflorescence 2 inches (5 cm) tall, with up to a dozen or more flowers. The species produces forms with other flower colors and forms with variegated foliage. Flowers last a month or two.

SEASON OF BLOOM: Summer to fall

MATURE PLANT: A dwarf plant from 3 to 6 inches (7.5–15 cm) tall. Forms multiple clumps. Foliage is keel shaped and 4–6 inches (10–15 cm) long.

EASE OF CULTURE: Intermediate

SUITABLE GROWING AREA: Windowsill, lights, greenhouse

LIGHT: Medium

TEMPERATURE: Intermediate to warm

RECOMMENDED POTTING MEDIUM: Mounted, in a basket in sphagnum moss, or in a cattleya mix in a pot

SPECIAL CULTURAL TIP: Reduce water in the winter.

COMMENT: Once the exclusive property of the royal family of Japan. Its cultivation dates many centuries back to the Edo Period in Japan. It was first described in 1784.

Phalaenopsis bellina

PRONUNCIATION: fal-en-OP-sis

AKA: *Phalaenopsis violacea* 'Borneo', *Phalaenopsis violacea* var. *bellina*

ORIGIN: Malaysia, East Malaysia

DESCRIPTION AND QUALITIES: A compact sweetly scented phalaenopsis that has both a beautiful flower and very attractive, glossy green foliage.

INTENSITY OF FRAGRANCE: Strong

WHEN FRAGRANT: Day

DESCRIPTION OF FRAGRANCE: Freesia, lily of the valley, rose, touch of velvet, lemon

FLOWER DESCRIPTION: Waxy, greenish flowers with purple markings, 2 inches (5 cm) across, borne sequentially. Inflorescence 4–6 inches (10–15 cm) tall, bearing three to four flowers.

SEASON OF BLOOM: Variable

MATURE PLANT: A compact grower with glossy green leaves 8–10 inches (20–25 cm) long.

Phalaenopsis bellina is used extensively as a parent to impart its waxy substance, color, and fragrance to its progeny.

Ease of culture: Intermediate

Suitable growing area: Windowsill, lights, greenhouse

Light: Low

Temperature: Warm

Recommended potting medium: Sphagnum moss, medium-textured bark, or coco chunk mix

Special cultural tip: Smaller seedling plants can be very susceptible to crown rot. Ensure that the growing point of the plant is dry going into the evening.

Comment: Discovered by Dutch botanist Johannes E. Teijsmann in 1859.

Phalaenopsis schilleriana

Pronunciation: fal-en-OP-sis

Aka: Sometimes spelled *Phalaenopsis schillerana*

Origin: Philippines

Description and qualities: Along with handsome silver-marked foliage, this species produces branching inflorescences of long-lasting pink flowers.

Intensity of fragrance: Light

When fragrant: Day

Description of fragrance: Rose

Flower description: Bright pink flowers 3–3^1/$_2$ inches (8–9 cm) wide. Inflorescence up to 3 feet (91 cm) long, with many flowers. It is reported that one plant had 733 blossoms! The flowers open at one time and therefore are not very long lasting.

Season of bloom: Winter to spring

Mature plant: Leaves are 6–18 inches (15–46 cm) long, mottled dark green above, entirely purple below.

Ease of culture: Easy

Suitable growing area: Windowsill, greenhouse

Light: Low

Temperature: Warm

Recommended potting medium: Medium-textured orchid mix, mounted on a slab or tree fern, or in a basket of sphagnum moss

Special cultural tip: Provide even moisture. Do not allow to dry out.

Comment: Named for the first grower of this species, Consul Schiller of Hamburg, Germany.

Even when *Phalaenopsis schilleriana* is not in bloom, its magnificent foliage alone makes it a stunner.

Rhynchostylis gigantea

PRONUNCIATION: rink-oh-STYE-liss
ORIGIN: Myanmar, Thailand, Vietnam
COMMON NAME: Foxtail orchid
FRAGRANT OFFSPRING: *Rhynchostylis* Winona Jordan (*Phalaenopsis* Doris ×
   Rhy. gigantea); *Vandachostylis* Azure (*Rhy. gigantea* × *Vanda coerulea*)

When *Rhynchostylis gigantea* is in bloom, its heady citrus fragrance can fill
a house.

DESCRIPTION AND QUALITIES: This species also produces solid red and pure white forms.

INTENSITY OF FRAGRANCE: Strong

WHEN FRAGRANT: Day

DESCRIPTION OF FRAGRANCE: Citrus

FLOWER DESCRIPTION: Flowers white with purple speckles, about 1 inch (2.5 cm) across. Inflorescence 15 inches (37.5 cm) long, bearing a multitude of flowers.

SEASON OF BLOOM: Fall to winter

MATURE PLANT: Slow growing, usually no taller than 12 inches (30 cm). Leaves can grow more than 12 inches (30 cm) long.

EASE OF CULTURE: Intermediate

SUITABLE GROWING AREA: Windowsill, greenhouse, lights

LIGHT: Medium

TEMPERATURE: Intermediate to warm

RECOMMENDED POTTING MEDIUM: Course-textured, well-drained mix

SPECIAL CULTURAL TIP: Resents frequent repotting. Often grown in slatted baskets.

COMMENT: Discovered in the 1830s in Myanmar by Danish physician and botanist Nathaniel Wallich.

OTHER FRAGRANT RHYNCHOSTYLIS: *Rhy. coelestis*—citrus; *Rhy. illustre*—citrus; *Rhy. retusa*—citrus.

Sedirea japonica is a delightful plant long highly admired by Asian orchid lovers for its delicate fragrance.

Sedirea japonica

PRONUNCIATION: se-DEER-ee-ah

ORIGIN: Japan, Korea

COMMON NAME: Yabukouji (Japanese)

FRAGRANT OFFSPRING: *Rhynchodirea* Dragon Charmy (*Sedirea japonica* × *Rhynchostylis gigantea*); *Vandirea* Newberry Jasmine (*Sedirea japonica* × *Vanda amesiana*)

DESCRIPTION AND QUALITIES: A delightful miniature from Asia that is finally receiving the attention and appreciation it deserves.

INTENSITY OF FRAGRANCE: Light

WHEN FRAGRANT: Day

DESCRIPTION OF FRAGRANCE: Fresh lemon

FLOWER DESCRIPTION: Cream to green

flowers with purple bars and spots on the lips and sepals. Flowers 1 inch (2.5 cm) across. Inflorescence 3–6 inches (8–15 cm) tall, with 3 to 12 flowers.

SEASON OF BLOOM: Spring to summer
MATURE PLANT: Miniature plant habit. Leaves about 6 inches (15 cm) long.
EASE OF CULTURE: Intermediate
SUITABLE GROWING AREA: Windowsill, lights, greenhouse
LIGHT: Medium
TEMPERATURE: Warm
RECOMMENDED POTTING MEDIUM: Sphagnum moss or a fine-textured phalaenopsis mix
SPECIAL CULTURAL TIP: Grow much like a phalaenopsis with slightly more light.
COMMENT: An orchid enjoyed and revered by the Japanese for hundreds of years is now starting to become more available to Western countries.

Trichoglottis philippinensis

PRONUNCIATION: trik-oh-GLOTT-iss
AKA: *Stauropsis philippinensis*
ORIGIN: Philippines
DESCRIPTION AND QUALITIES: A striking plant with attractive, unique flowers.
INTENSITY OF FRAGRANCE: Light
WHEN FRAGRANT: Day
DESCRIPTION OF FRAGRANCE: Ripe apples
FLOWER DESCRIPTION: Dark burgundy flowers with a bright pink lip. Flowers are 1–1^1/$_2$ inches (2.5–4 cm) wide, borne singly from the axils of the leaves. The species produces color forms ranging from brown to dark burgundy.
SEASON OF BLOOM: Spring to summer
MATURE PLANT: A slow grower up to 48 inches (90 cm) high. Can be topped to keep it short. Leaves tightly arranged on the stem.
EASE OF CULTURE: Intermediate
SUITABLE GROWING AREA: Windowsill, lights, greenhouse

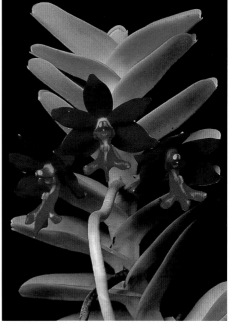

Trichoglottis philippinensis 'Pololei' is a curious plant with the delicious scent of ripe fruit.
PHOTO BY MARC HERZOG.

LIGHT: Medium
TEMPERATURE: Intermediate
RECOMMENDED POTTING MEDIUM: Medium-textured orchid mix
COMMENT: Described in 1845 by John Lindley.
OTHER FRAGRANT TRICHOGLOTTIS: *Trgl. wenzellii*—sweet

Tuberolabium kotoense
PRONUNCIATION: too-burr-oh-LAY-bee-um
AKA: *Saccolabium quisumbingii*
ORIGIN: Southeast Asia including Taiwan and Philippines
DESCRIPTION AND QUALITIES: An easy-to-grow species commonly found on *Ficus* trees in mountainous areas of Taiwan and the Philippines.
INTENSITY OF FRAGRANCE: Strong
WHEN FRAGRANT: Day
DESCRIPTION OF FRAGRANCE: Floral
FLOWER DESCRIPTION: Small, white, long-lasting, waxy flowers with purple-tipped lips. Flowers $\frac{1}{2}$ inch (1 cm) across. Inflorescence 2–3 inches (5–7.5 cm) tall, with 50 or more flowers per spike as the plant matures.
SEASON OF BLOOM: Fall to winter
MATURE PLANT: Dwarf grower.
EASE OF CULTURE: Easy
SUITABLE GROWING AREA: Windowsill, lights, greenhouse

The diminutive *Tuberolabium kotoense* can display up to 50 small, sweetly scented flowers on a single plant.

LIGHT: Medium
TEMPERATURE: Intermediate to warm
RECOMMENDED POTTING MEDIUM: Mounted on a slab, in medium-textured
   bark, or in coco chunks mix in a pot
OTHER FRAGRANT TUBEROLABIUMS: *Tblm. odoratissium*—sweet

Vanda denisoniana
PRONUNCIATION: VAN-da
ORIGIN: Myanmar
FRAGRANT OFFSPRING: *Aeridovanda* Kinnaree (*Vanda denisoniana* × *Aerides
lawrenceae*)
DESCRIPTION AND QUALITIES: A compact grower with many color forms.
INTENSITY OF FRAGRANCE: Strong
WHEN FRAGRANT: Evening
DESCRIPTION OF FRAGRANCE: Sweet
FLOWER DESCRIPTION: Flower 2 inches (5 cm) across. Yellow petals and
   sepals with light spotting. Center of flower is white. Inflorescence 6
   inches (15 cm) tall, bearing four to six flowers.
SEASON OF BLOOM: Spring
MATURE PLANT: Spreads about 12 inches (30 cm) but takes several years to
   reach 12 inches (30 cm) tall.
EASE OF CULTURE: Intermediate
SUITABLE GROWING AREA: Windowsill, greenhouse
LIGHT: Medium to high
TEMPERATURE: Warm
RECOMMENDED POTTING MEDIUM: Coarse-textured mix
SPECIAL CULTURAL TIP: Fre-
quently grown in wooden
baskets with or without
media.
COMMENT: Often used in breeding vandas for its yellow color
and erect flower spike.
OTHER FRAGRANT VANDAS:
V. coerulescens—grape bubblegum, concord grapes; *V.
cristata*—floral; *V. dearei*—
vanilla, cinnamon; *V. roeblingiana*—sweet; *V. tesselata*—
grapes, lilac; *V. tricolor* var.
suavis—vanilla; *V. tricolor*—
vanilla.

Several species of vandas, including *Vanda
denisoniana*, are pleasantly fragrant.

Hybrids

Angranthes Grandalena

PRONUNCIATION: an-GRAN-theez
ORIGIN: *Angraecum magdalenae* × *Aeranthes grandiflora*
FRAGRANT PARENTS: Both parents
DESCRIPTION AND QUALITIES: As this plant matures, it produces multiple
   growths with recurring, almost constant, blooming.
INTENSITY OF FRAGRANCE: Strong
WHEN FRAGRANT: Evening
DESCRIPTION OF FRAGRANCE: Jasmine
FLOWER DESCRIPTION: Greenish white spurred flowers 3 inches (7.5 cm)
   across. Inflorescence 10–12 inches (25–30 cm) tall, with one flower.
SEASON OF BLOOM: Variable
MATURE PLANT: A compact plant, 8–10 inches (20–24 cm) tall. Forms addi-
   tional plants at base. Foliage dark green and glossy.
EASE OF CULTURE: Easy

Because of its ease of culture and frequency of
blooming, *Angranthes* Grandalena has become
one of my favorites angraecoids.

SUITABLE GROWING AREA: Windowsill,
   lights, greenhouse
LIGHT: Medium
TEMPERATURE: Intermediate
RECOMMENDED POTTING MEDIUM:
   Medium-textured orchid bark or
   coco chunk mix
SPECIAL CULTURAL TIP: Like most
   angraecoids, this plant resents
   repotting.
COMMENT: Hybridized by orchid
   grower and author Fred Hillerman
   in 1979.

Neostylis Lou Sneary 'Pinky'
AM/AOS
PRONUNCIATION: nee-oh-STYE-liss
ORIGIN: *Neofinetia falcata* × *Rhyncho-
   stylis coelestis*
FRAGRANT PARENTS: Both parents
DESCRIPTION AND QUALITIES: A very
   compact growing orchid perfect for
   windowsills and under lights.
INTENSITY OF FRAGRANCE: Light
WHEN FRAGRANT: Day

DESCRIPTION OF FRAGRANCE: Vanilla, candy

FLOWER DESCRIPTION: Clouds of 1-inch (2.5-cm) wide, deliciously fragrant, creamy white flowers richly marked in pink, with bright fuchsia pink lips. Inflorescence 6–8 inches (15–20 cm) tall, bearing many flowers.

SEASON OF BLOOM: Variable

MATURE PLANT: Very compact growing.

EASE OF CULTURE: Easy

SUITABLE GROWING AREA: Windowsill, lights, greenhouse

LIGHT: Medium

TEMPERATURE: Intermediate to warm

RECOMMENDED POTTING MEDIUM: Fine-textured mix

SPECIAL CULTURAL TIP: Grow in pots or baskets.

COMMENT: Orchid suppliers are beginning to provide *Neostylis* crosses, of which the Lou Sneary grex is one of the most popular.

OTHER FRAGRANT NEOSTYLIS: *Neost.* Lou Sneary 'Blue Moon'—jasmine; *Neost.* Lou Sneary—vanilla, candy.

Neostylis Lou Sneary is a floriferous prize-winning grex.

Phalaenopsis Caribbean Sunset 'Sweet Fragrance' is a delightful, dwarf, red phalaenopsis hybrid with a delicate, roselike scent.

Phalaenopsis Caribbean Sunset 'Sweet Fragrance'

PRONUNCIATION: fal-en-OP-sis
ORIGIN: *Phalaenopsis* Cassandra × *Phalaenopsis* Mambo
FRAGRANT PARENTS: Both parents
DESCRIPTION AND QUALITIES: A sweet-smelling, charming miniature phalaenopsis.
INTENSITY OF FRAGRANCE: Light
WHEN FRAGRANT: Day
DESCRIPTION OF FRAGRANCE: Rose floral
FLOWER DESCRIPTION: Rose-red flowers 2 inches (5 cm) across. Inflorescence 6 inches (15 cm) tall, with many flowers.
SEASON OF BLOOM: Variable
MATURE PLANT: Dwarf. Leaves 6 inches (15 cm) long.
EASE OF CULTURE: Easy
SUITABLE GROWING AREA: Windowsill, lights, greenhouse
LIGHT: Low
TEMPERATURE: Warm
RECOMMENDED POTTING MEDIUM: Medium-textured mix
COMMENT: Part of a series of fragrant phalaenopsis bred by Norman's Orchids.

Phalaenopsis Ember 'Blumen Insel' AM/AOS

PRONUNCIATION: fal-en-OP-sis
ORIGIN: *Phalaenopsis* Mahalo 'Carmella' FCC/AOS × *Phalaenopsis* George Vasquez 'Eureka' FCC/AOS
FRAGRANT PARENTS: Both parents
DESCRIPTION AND QUALITIES: Gorgeous foliage and flowers distinguish this orchid.
INTENSITY OF FRAGRANCE: Light
WHEN FRAGRANT: Day
DESCRIPTION OF FRAGRANCE: Rose floral
FLOWER DESCRIPTION: Glossy, waxy solid dark red flowers 2$^1/_2$ inches (6.5 cm) wide. Inflorescence thick and stiff, 12 inches (30 cm) tall, with five to six flowers. Blooms more than one time per year.
SEASON OF BLOOM: Variable

MATURE PLANT: Leaves broad and long, 10–12 inches (26–30 cm).
EASE OF CULTURE: Easy
SUITABLE GROWING AREA: Windowsill, lights, greenhouse
LIGHT: Low
TEMPERATURE: Warm
RECOMMENDED POTTING MEDIUM: Medium-textured orchid mix

Phalaenopsis Kilby Cassviola 'Sweet Fragrance'

PRONUNCIATION: fal-en-OP-sis
ORIGIN: *Phalaenopsis* Cassandra × *Phalaenopsis violacea*
FRAGRANT PARENTS: *Phalaenopsis violacea*
DESCRIPTION AND QUALITIES: A superb combination of a flurry of white flowers on a compact plant with beautifully marbled foliage.
INTENSITY OF FRAGRANCE: Light
WHEN FRAGRANT: Day
DESCRIPTION OF FRAGRANCE: Spicy
FLOWER DESCRIPTION: Clear white flowers with a yellow flush and light brown barring on the lower sepals and throat. Flowers 2½ inches (6 cm) wide. Inflorescence 12 inches (30 cm) tall, bearing 5–10 flowers.
SEASON OF BLOOM: Variable
MATURE PLANT: A very compact grower.
EASE OF CULTURE: Intermediate
SUITABLE GROWING AREA: Windowsill, lights, greenhouse
LIGHT: Low
TEMPERATURE: Warm
RECOMMENDED POTTING MEDIUM: Medium-textured mix
COMMENT: Part of a series of fragrant phalaenopsis bred by Norman's Orchids.

Phalaenopsis Ember 'Blumen Insel' AM/AOS makes a perfect houseplant with its waxy, dark red, lightly rose scented flowers and dark green, glossy leaves.

Phalaenopsis Kilby Cassviola 'Sweet Fragrance' produces glistening white, spicy scented flowers.

Phalaenopsis Mini Mark is a darling miniature orchid that some growers claim has a delicate floral scent while others cannot detect it.
PHOTO BY MARC HERZOG.

Phalaenopsis Mini Mark 'Maria Teresa'

PRONUNCIATION: fal-en-OP-sis

ORIGIN: *Phalaenopsis* Micro Nova × *Phalaenopsis philippinensis*

DESCRIPTION AND QUALITIES: A delightful phalaenopsis that everyone has space for. Some clones of the grex Mini Mark are fragrant, others are not.

INTENSITY OF FRAGRANCE: Light

WHEN FRAGRANT: Day

DESCRIPTION OF FRAGRANCE: Sweet floral

FLOWER DESCRIPTION: White flowers with dark red speckles and orange and yellow lips. Flowers 1¼ inches (3 cm) wide. Inflorescence 3–4 inches (7.5–10 cm) tall, bearing four to six flowers.

SEASON OF BLOOM: Variable

MATURE PLANT: A miniature habit.

EASE OF CULTURE: Easy

SUITABLE GROWING AREA: Windowsill, lights, greenhouse

LIGHT: Low to medium

TEMPERATURE: Warm

RECOMMENDED POTTING MEDIUM: Medium-textured epiphytic orchid mix

Phalaenopsis Orchid World 'Roman Holiday' AM/AOS

PRONUNCIATION: fal-en-OP-sis

ORIGIN: *Phalaenopsis* Malibu Imp × *Phalaenopsis* Deventeriana

FRAGRANT PARENTS: *Phalaenopsis* Deventeriana

DESCRIPTION AND QUALITIES: All cultivars in the grex Orchid World are noted for their fabulous fragrance.

INTENSITY OF FRAGRANCE: Strong

WHEN FRAGRANT: Day

DESCRIPTION OF FRAGRANCE: Spicy

FLOWER DESCRIPTION: Impressive, yellow flowers with red bars. Flowers 2½ inches (6 cm) across and of a heavy substance. Inflorescence 12 inches (30 cm) tall, bearing five to six flowers.

SEASON OF BLOOM: Spring

MATURE PLANT: Average phalaenopsis size, that is, with a leaf spread of 12 inches (30 cm).

EASE OF CULTURE: Easy

SUITABLE GROWING AREA: Windowsill, greenhouse, lights

LIGHT: Low to medium

TEMPERATURE: Warm

RECOMMENDED POTTING MEDIUM: Medium-textured bark or coco chunk mix in northern climates. High quality sphagnum moss in warmer, drier growing areas.

OTHER FRAGRANT PHALAENOPSIS: *Phal.* Orchid World 'Bonnie Vasquez' AM/AOS—spicy

Phalaenopsis Perfection Is 'Chen' FCC/AOS

PRONUNCIATION: fal-en-OP-sis

ORIGIN: *Phalaenopsis* Golden Peoker × *Phalaenopsis* Black Eagle

DESCRIPTION AND QUALITIES: One of my favorite small-growing, fragrant phalaenopsis.

INTENSITY OF FRAGRANCE: Strong

WHEN FRAGRANT: Day

DESCRIPTION OF FRAGRANCE: Spicy, cloves, carnation

FLOWER DESCRIPTION: Flat yellow flowers of heavy substance covered with burgundy red spots. Flowers $2^{1}/_{2}$ inches (6.5 cm) wide.

SEASON OF BLOOM: Variable

MATURE PLANT: A compact phalaenopsis.

EASE OF CULTURE: Easy

SUITABLE GROWING AREA: Windowsill, greenhouse, lights

LIGHT: Low

TEMPERATURE: Warm

RECOMMENDED POTTING MEDIUM: Medium-textured orchid mix or sphagnum moss

Phalaenopsis Orchid World 'Roman Holiday' AM/AOS is one of many fine-colored and sweet-scented cultivars in its grex.

Phalaenopsis Perfection Is 'Chen' FCC/AOS is a gorgeous, flat, waxy, bright flower with a strong, spicy scent. PHOTO BY MARC HERZOG.

Phalaenopsis Sweet Memory 'Amy Dawn' AM/AOS

PRONUNCIATION: fal-en-OP-sis
ORIGIN: *Phalaenopsis* Deventeriana × *Phalaenopsis violacea*
FRAGRANT PARENTS: Both parents
DESCRIPTION AND QUALITIES: Makes a spectacular specimen plant and has long-lasting flowers.
INTENSITY OF FRAGRANCE: Strong
WHEN FRAGRANT: Day
DESCRIPTION OF FRAGRANCE: Freesia

Phalaenopsis Sweet Memory 'Amy Dawn' AM/AOS, like all members of its grex, has delightful fragrance. PHOTO BY ERIC GOO FROM BUD TERRELL'S COLLECTION.

FLOWER DESCRIPTION: Rich pink flowers strongly resembling *Phalaenopsis violacea* in shape but with broader petals and sepals. Flowers 3 inches (7.6 cm) wide. Inflorescence 12–14 inches (30–40 cm) tall, bearing six to eight flowers.

SEASON OF BLOOM: Spring

MATURE PLANT: Forms *keikis* (baby plants) at its base, providing the potential to become a large specimen plant. Standard phalaenopsis size, that is, with a leaf spread of 12 inches (30 cm).

EASE OF CULTURE: Easy

SUITABLE GROWING AREA: Windowsill, lights, greenhouse

LIGHT: Low

TEMPERATURE: Warm

RECOMMENDED POTTING MEDIUM: Medium-textured orchid mix or sphagnum moss

Phalaenopsis Valentinii

PRONUNCIATION: fal-en-OP-sis

ORIGIN: *Phalaenopsis violacea* × *Phalaenopsis cornu-cervi*

FRAGRANT PARENTS: *Phalaenopsis violacea*

DESCRIPTION AND QUALITIES: Another phalaenopsis noted for its fine foliage and fragrant, colorful flowers.

INTENSITY OF FRAGRANCE: Light

WHEN FRAGRANT: Day

DESCRIPTION OF FRAGRANCE: Freesia

FLOWER DESCRIPTION: Glossy, waxy, violet over brown flowers with purple lips and yellow in the throats. Flowers 2$^{1}\!/_{2}$ inches (6 cm) wide. Inflorescence 6 inches (15 cm) tall, bearing three to four flowers.

SEASON OF BLOOM: Variable

MATURE PLANT: A compact grower.

EASE OF CULTURE: Easy

SUITABLE GROWING AREA: Windowsill, lights, greenhouse

LIGHT: Low

TEMPERATURE: Warm

RECOMMENDED POTTING MEDIUM: Medium-textured orchid mix or sphagnum moss

The primary hybrid *Phalaenopsis* Valentinii has varnished flat flowers with the freesia scent from its *Phalaenopsis violacea* parent.

Vanda Pat Delight is a huge luscious hybrid that smells like ripe grapes.

Vanda Pat Delight
PRONUNCIATION: VAN-da
ORIGIN: *Vanda* Kasem's Delight ×
    Vanda Fuch's Delight
DESCRIPTION AND QUALITIES: One of
    the best blue-purple vandas.
INTENSITY OF FRAGRANCE: Light
WHEN FRAGRANT: Day
DESCRIPTION OF FRAGRANCE: Ripe
    grapes
FLOWER DESCRIPTION: Impressive deep
    purple blooms 5 inches (12 cm)
    across. Inflorescence 24 inches (60
    cm) tall, bearing 6 to 10 flowers.
SEASON OF BLOOM: Variable
MATURE PLANT: Standard vanda size,
    that is, with a leaf spread of 12
    inches (30 cm).
EASE OF CULTURE: Intermediate
SUITABLE GROWING AREA: Windowsill,
    greenhouse
LIGHT: Medium to high
TEMPERATURE: Intermediate to warm
RECOMMENDED POTTING MEDIUM: In a basket. Will grow in a course-tex-
    tured mix in a pot

Vascostylis Crownfox Red Gem
PRONUNCIATION: vass-coh-STYE-liss
ORIGIN: *Rhynchostylis gigantea* 'Red' × *Ascocenda* Red Gem
FRAGRANT PARENTS: *Rhynchostylis gigantea*
DESCRIPTION AND QUALITIES: Combines fragrance from its rhynchostylis
    parent with the compact growth habit of its ascocenda parent.
INTENSITY OF FRAGRANCE: Strong
WHEN FRAGRANT: Day
DESCRIPTION OF FRAGRANCE: Citrus
FLOWER DESCRIPTION: Cranberry red, long-lasting flowers 1^{3}/4 inches (4 cm)
    across. Inflorescence 12 inches (30 cm) tall, bearing 10–12 flowers.
SEASON OF BLOOM: Variable
MATURE PLANT: Average ascocenda size, that is, about 10 inches (25 cm)
    across.
EASE OF CULTURE: Intermediate

Vascostylis Crownfox Red Gem produces an alluring citrus scent.

SUITABLE GROWING AREA: Windowsill, greenhouse
LIGHT: Medium
TEMPERATURE: Intermediate to warm
RECOMMENDED POTTING MEDIUM: In a basket or in a medium-textured, well-drained mix
OTHER FRAGRANT VASCOSTYLIS: *Vasco*. Tham Yuen Hae 'Blue Queen' HCC/RSPC, JC/AOS, HCC/AOS—jasmine

Chapter 8

Other Orchids

Some orchid genera are comprised of only a smattering of fragrant species and hybrids. They include members of the subfamily Epidendrum, tribe Maxillaria, the slipper orchids (*Paphiopedilum* and *Phragmipedium*), the Pleurothallid Alliance, and a group that I am calling the "Stinkers". As I have mentioned earlier, the focus of this book is pleasant-smelling orchids, not malodorous ones, but I feel it is necessary to mention at least a few of these. For those so inclined, here are a few other plants, not profiled, that fit in this group: *Bulbophyllum beccarii*, *Bulb. echinolabium*, *Bulb. maximum*, *Bulb. phalaenopsis*, *Cirrhopetalum graveolens*. *Cirr. ornatissimum*, *Eria hyacinthoides*, *Gongora grossa*, *Masdevallia triangularis*, *Oncidium crispum*, and *Pleurothallis cocornaensis*. You can check out details about them in the various appendices.

Subfamily Epidendrum Species

Ansellia africana
PRONUNCIATION: an-SELL-ee-a
AKA: *Ansellia gigantea*
ORIGIN: Africa
COMMON NAME: Leopard orchid
DESCRIPTION AND QUALITIES: Has best fragrance under very high light conditions.
INTENSITY OF FRAGRANCE: Light
WHEN FRAGRANT: Day
DESCRIPTION OF FRAGRANCE: Light floral
FLOWER DESCRIPTION: Yellowish flowers with brown spots. Flowers 1½–2 inches (3–5 cm) across. Inflorescence a branched spike, up to 3 feet (90 cm) tall, bearing up to 100 flowers.
SEASON OF BLOOM: Spring to summer

MATURE PLANT: Very large plant with pseudobulbs up to 2 feet (60 cm) long and leaves about 5 inches (12.5 cm) long.

EASE OF CULTURE: Intermediate

SUITABLE GROWING AREA: Greenhouse

LIGHT: High

TEMPERATURE: Warm

RECOMMENDED POTTING MEDIUM: Medium-textured mix

SPECIAL CULTURAL TIP: Keep damp during the growing season. Reduce water slightly when not actively growing.

COMMENT: Named for English gardener John Ansell who discovered this plant on an expedition to Niger in 1840.

The prominently marked flowers of *Ansellia africana* explain its common name, the leopard orchid.

Arundina graminifolia

PRONUNCIATION: a-run-DEE-na

AKA: *Bletia graminifolia, Arundina bambusifolia*

ORIGIN: Southeast Asia

COMMON NAME: Bamboo orchid

DESCRIPTION AND QUALITIES: An orchid that requires a lot of space.

INTENSITY OF FRAGRANCE: Light

WHEN FRAGRANT: Day

DESCRIPTION OF FRAGRANCE: Floral

FLOWER DESCRIPTION: Flower 3 inches (7.5 cm) across, usually rosy mauve but color is variable, short lived (usually three to four days). Inflorescence 4–6 feet (120–180 cm) tall, bearing two to six flowers.

SEASON OF BLOOM: Spring

MATURE PLANT: The slender, upright stems grow in clusters.

EASE OF CULTURE: Easy

SUITABLE GROWING AREA: Greenhouse

LIGHT: High

Arundina graminifolia is commonly grown as a "garden orchid" in the tropics.

TEMPERATURE: Warm
RECOMMENDED POTTING MEDIUM: Terrestrial mix in a large pot or directly
   in ground
SPECIAL CULTURAL TIP: Grow in beds or large pots.
COMMENT: Originally described in 1825 by David Don as *Bletia graminifolia*.

Coelogyne lawrenceana
PRONUNCIATION: see-LOJ-in-ee
ORIGIN: Vietnam
DESCRIPTION AND QUALITIES: A very vigorous-growing species.
INTENSITY OF FRAGRANCE: Light
WHEN FRAGRANT: Day
DESCRIPTION OF FRAGRANCE: Sweet floral
FLOWER DESCRIPTION: Waxy, tan flowers with white lips. Flowers $3^1/_2$ inches
   (9 cm) across. Inflorescence 10 inches (25 cm), bearing one to three
   flowers.
SEASON OF BLOOM: Spring to summer
MATURE PLANT: Soft, pleated foliage about 12 inches (30 cm) high.
EASE OF CULTURE: Intermediate
SUITABLE GROWING AREA: Greenhouse, windowsill, lights
LIGHT: Medium
TEMPERATURE: Warm
RECOMMENDED POTTING MEDIUM: Medium-textured mix
SPECIAL CULTURAL TIP: Repot before new growth begins.

Coelogyne lawrenceana is an uncommon and sought-after species from Vietnam.

Coelogyne ochracea

PRONUNCIATION: see-LOJ-in-ee

ORIGIN: India

DESCRIPTION AND QUALITIES: The most popular species in this genus because it is easy to grow, very fragrant, and compact in habit.

INTENSITY OF FRAGRANCE: Light

WHEN FRAGRANT: Day

DESCRIPTION OF FRAGRANCE: Musk

FLOWER DESCRIPTION: Pure white flowers with striking yellow and orange markings on the lip. Flowers $1^1/4$ inches (4 cm) wide. Inflorescence 8 inches (20 cm) tall, bearing 6 to 10 flowers.

SEASON OF BLOOM: Spring

MATURE PLANT: Reaches 8 inches (20 cm) tall.

EASE OF CULTURE: Easy

SUITABLE GROWING AREA: Windowsill, greenhouse

LIGHT: Medium

TEMPERATURE: Cool

RECOMMENDED POTTING MEDIUM: Medium-textured mix

COMMENT: This species does not lose its leaves during the winter.

OTHER FRAGRANT COELOGYNES: *Coel. cristata*—banana, candy sweet; *Coel. fimbriata*—yeasty; *Coel.* Intermedia—sweet, fruity; *Coel. pandurata*—cinnamon; *Coel. zurowetzii*—spicy floral.

Coelogyne ochracea sports crisp white flowers with bright yellow and orange markings on the lip and in the throat.

Hybrids

Catasetum Orchidglade 'Davie Ranches' AM/AOS

PRONUNCIATION: kat-a-SEE-tum

ORIGIN: *Catasetum pileatum* × *Catasetum expansum*

DESCRIPTION AND QUALITIES: As is the case with most catasetums, the male flowers have a stronger scent than the female flowers. The fragrance of the blossoms remains, to some degree, even after the flowers dry, making them useful for potpourri. Flowers are most fragrant in warm sunlight.

INTENSITY OF FRAGRANCE: Strong

WHEN FRAGRANT: Day

DESCRIPTION OF FRAGRANCE: Spicy, medicinal

FLOWER DESCRIPTION: Creamy, thick, waxy flowers covered with red freckles. Flowers 2 inches (5 cm) across. Inflorescence 6–8 inches (15–20 cm) tall, with up to 15 flowers.

SEASON OF BLOOM: Summer to fall

MATURE PLANT: Leaves deciduous, 12–16 inches (30–40 cm) long.

EASE OF CULTURE: Intermediate

SUITABLE GROWING AREA: Windowsill, greenhouse

LIGHT: Medium

TEMPERATURE: Intermediate

RECOMMENDED POTTING MEDIUM: In a basket so plants will have rapid drainage.

SPECIAL CULTURAL TIP: Water and fertilize heavily during the growing season. Stop water for four to six weeks during the winter.

COMMENT: The first commercial *Catasetum* hybrid. Created by Jones and Scully, commercial orchid growers in Miami.

OTHER FRAGRANT CATASETUMS: *Ctsm. candida*—wintergreen; *Ctsm. collare*—wintergreen; *Ctsm. discolor*—rye bread; *Ctsm. expansum*—turpentine in morning; rye bread in afternoon; *Ctsm. fimbriatum*—spice; *Ctsm. gnomus*—wintergreen; *Ctsm. integerrimum*—spice; *Ctsm. maculatum*—rye bread; *Ctsm. roseum*—

Catasetum Orchidglade 'Davie Ranches' AM/AOS has rich color and fragrance.

Vicks VapoRub in the morning, cinnamon at night; Ctsm. tenebrosum—citrus; Ctsm. warscewiczii—lemon.

Cymbidium Golden Elf 'Sundust' HCC/AOS

PRONUNCIATION: sim-BID-ee-um
ORIGIN: *Cymbidium ensifolium* × *Cymbidium* Enid Haupt
FRAGRANT PARENTS: *Cymbidium ensifolium*
DESCRIPTION AND QUALITIES: The clear golden yellow, sweetly fragrant flowers on a compact plant make this miniature cymbidium a favorite.
INTENSITY OF FRAGRANCE: Light
WHEN FRAGRANT: Day
DESCRIPTION OF FRAGRANCE: Rose
FLOWER DESCRIPTION: Clear bright yellow flowers $2^{1}/_{2}$ inches (6 cm) across. Inflorescence a spike, with four to six flowers. Can bloom several times a year. Flowers last about two weeks.
SEASON OF BLOOM: Summer to fall
MATURE PLANT: Considered a miniature cymbidium.
EASE OF CULTURE: Intermediate
SUITABLE GROWING AREA: Windowsill, greenhouse
LIGHT: High
TEMPERATURE: Intermediate
RECOMMENDED POTTING MEDIUM: Terrestrial mix.
SPECIAL CULTURAL TIP: Requires less cooling than most other cymbidiums to initiate buds. This makes it easier to bloom than many other cymbidiums. More heat tolerant than most cymbidiums so it is suited for warmer climates.
OTHER FRAGRANT CYMBIDIUMS: *Cym. cyperifolium*—sweet; *Cym. eburneum*—sweet, like paperwhite narcissus; *Cym. goeringii*—jasmine, lily-of-the valley, lemons; *Cym. kanran*—lemon peel; *Cym. mastersii*—almonds; *Cym. sinensis*—light, sweet floral; *Cym. suave*—sweet; *Cym. virescens*—the sweet, delicate fragrance earned it the moniker of "the scent of the king."

Cymbidium Golden Elf 'Sundust' HCC/AOS is a compact, warm-tolerant, fragrant hybrid.

Tribe Maxillaria Species

Bifrenaria harrisoniae

PRONUNCIATION: bye-fren-AIR-ee-a
AKA: *Dendrobium harrisoniae*
ORIGIN: Brazil
DESCRIPTION AND QUALITIES: The long-lasting very fragrant flower is the prime feature of this orchid.
INTENSITY OF FRAGRANCE: Strong

Bifrenaria harrisoniae features waxy white flowers with a sweet scent.

WHEN FRAGRANT: Day
DESCRIPTION OF FRAGRANCE: Fruity
FLOWER DESCRIPTION: Waxy, fleshy, usually white flowers that last up to six weeks. Flowers 2–3 inches (5–7 cm) across. Inflorescence 2 inches (5 cm) tall, with one to two flowers.
SEASON OF BLOOM: Spring
MATURE PLANT: Pseudobulbs 2–3 inches (5–7.5 cm) long. Leaves 8–10 inches (20–30 cm) long.
EASE OF CULTURE: Intermediate
SUITABLE GROWING AREA: Windowsill, greenhouse
LIGHT: Medium
TEMPERATURE: Intermediate
RECOMMENDED POTTING MEDIUM: Medium-textured epiphytic mix
SPECIAL CULTURAL TIP: Needs no rest period. Reduce water during winter to improve bud set. Divide sparingly.
COMMENT: Sent to England from Rio de Janeiro by W. Harrison in the 1820s.

Cochleanthes amazonica

PRONUNCIATION: kok-lee-AN-theez
ORIGIN: Costa Rica, Panama
FRAGRANT OFFSPRING: *Cochleanthes* Moliere (*Cnths. discolor* × *Cnths. amazonica*); *Cochleanthes* Amazing (*Cnths. flabelliformis* × *Cnths. amazonica*)

The exotic flower of *Cochleanthes amazonica* is made more exciting with dark purple veins on the impressive lip and in the throat.

DESCRIPTION AND QUALITIES: The large dramatically marked lip makes this orchid stand out.

INTENSITY OF FRAGRANCE: Very strong

WHEN FRAGRANT: Day

DESCRIPTION OF FRAGRANCE: Candy, rose, narcissus, verbena

FLOWER DESCRIPTION: White flowers with contrasting dark purple veins on very prominent lips and in the throats. Flowers 2 inches (5 cm) across. Inflorescence 3 inches (7.5 cm) tall, bearing one flower.

SEASON OF BLOOM: Winter to spring

MATURE PLANT: Reaches 8 inches (20 cm) tall.

EASE OF CULTURE: Intermediate

SUITABLE GROWING AREA: Windowsill, lights, greenhouse

LIGHT: Low to medium

TEMPERATURE: Intermediate

RECOMMENDED POTTING MEDIUM: Fine-textured, well-drained mix

SPECIAL CULTURAL TIP: Keep the growing medium damp to avoid pleating of the foliage. Make sure potting mix is fresh and not broken down as this plant does not tolerate a soggy medium.

OTHER FRAGRANT COCHLEANTHES: *Cnths. discolor*—candy, cedar, pepper, camphoraceous

Lycaste aromatica

PRONUNCIATION: lye-KASS-tee

AKA: *Colax aromaticus, Lycaste suaveolens*

ORIGIN: Mexico

DESCRIPTION AND QUALITIES: This is a deciduous orchid that drops its leaves in the winter. It blooms before the plant grows new foliage in the early spring.

INTENSITY OF FRAGRANCE: Very strong

WHEN FRAGRANT: Day

DESCRIPTION OF FRAGRANCE: Cinnamon, spicy, like Big Red chewing gum

FLOWER DESCRIPTION: Bright yellow-orange flowers $2^{1}/_{2}$ inches (6 cm) wide. Inflorescence 6 inches (15 cm) tall, bearing flowers in groups of 30 to 40 from previous year's growth or on new growth.

SEASON OF BLOOM: Spring

MATURE PLANT: Leaves 12–16 inches (30-40 cm) long, soft and pleated.

Lycaste aromatica has a compact plant habit with cheery, bright cinnamon-scented yellow-orange flowers. Photo by Allen Black.

EASE OF CULTURE: Easy

SUITABLE GROWING AREA: Windowsill, lights, greenhouse

LIGHT: Medium to high

TEMPERATURE: Cool to intermediate

RECOMMENDED POTTING MEDIUM: In a clay pot with a mix of rock wool and perlite, or in bark

SPECIAL CULTURAL TIP: Reduce water during the winter. Mist occasionally to keep the pseudobulbs from shriveling. More intense light results in richer flower color.

COMMENT: One of the easier to grow and rewarding lycastes. First collected by Lord Napier in Mexico and sent to the Royal Botanic Garden in Edinburgh, where it flowered in 1826.

OTHER FRAGRANT LYCASTES: *Lyc.* Alan Salzman—spicy; *Lyc. bradeorum*—lemon; *Lyc. brevispatha*—fresh apples; *Lyc. ciliata*—ripe apples; *Lyc. cochleata*—oranges; *Lyc. cruenta*—spicy, cinnamon, lemon, cloves; *Lyc. deppei*—peppermint, eucalyptus; *Lyc. lanipes*—heady, honey perfume; *Lyc. leucantha*—sweet, heady perfume; *Lyc. locusta*—Granny Smith apples; *Lyc. powellii*—sweet floral; *Lyc.* Walnut Valley 'Black's Glow'—spicy.

Maxillaria tenuifolia

PRONUNCIATION: mak-si-LAIR-ee-a

AKA: *Maxillaria gracilifolia*

ORIGIN: Mexico to Costa Rica

COMMON NAME: Coconut orchid

DESCRIPTION AND QUALITIES: Found in semi-deciduous forests at low elevations. One of the most popular of the 200 or so *Maxillaria* species.

INTENSITY OF FRAGRANCE: Strong

WHEN FRAGRANT: Day

DESCRIPTION OF FRAGRANCE: Coconut; box of crayons

FLOWER DESCRIPTION: Brick red flowers $1\frac{1}{2}$–2 inches (4–5 cm) across. Inflorescence 4–5 inches (10–12.5 cm) tall, with one flower.

SEASON OF BLOOM: Summer

MATURE PLANT: Reaches 10 inches (25 cm) high.

EASE OF CULTURE: Easy

SUITABLE GROWING AREA: Windowsill, lights, greenhouse

LIGHT: Medium

TEMPERATURE: Intermediate

RECOMMENDED POTTING MEDIUM: Mounted on a raft or slab. Can be grown in pots with a mixture of well-draining media like shredded tree fern.

SPECIAL CULTURAL TIP: Keep moist.

COMMENT: Discovered in Veracruz, Mexico, by German orchid collector Karl Theodor Hartweg in 1837.

OTHER FRAGRANT MAXILLARIAS: *Max. ochroleuca*—tutti-frutti; *Max. picta*—sweet floral; *Max. rufescens*—vanilla, egg crème; *Max. sanderiana*—sweet floral; *Max. seymouriana*—lemony.

No one can resist the mouthwatering coconut fragrance of *Maxillaria tenuifolia*.

Tribe Maxillaria Hybrids

Cochleanthes Moliere is a spectacular result of the marriage of two species.

Cochleanthes Moliere

PRONUNCIATION: kok-lee-AN-theez
ORIGIN: *Cochleanthes amazonica* × *Cochleanthes discolor*
FRAGRANT PARENTS: Both parents
DESCRIPTION AND QUALITIES: The gorgeous, huge royal purple lip and candy sweet fragrance combined with easy phalaenopsis-like culture has made this hybrid a hit.
INTENSITY OF FRAGRANCE: Strong
WHEN FRAGRANT: Day
DESCRIPTION OF FRAGRANCE: Candy, rose
FLOWER DESCRIPTION: White petals and sepals tipped with pink contrast with the huge dramatic purple lip. Flowers 2 inches (5 cm) across. Inflorescence 3–5 inches (8–12.5 cm) tall, with a single flower.
SEASON OF BLOOM: Variable
MATURE PLANT: Reaches 8 inches (20 cm) tall.
EASE OF CULTURE: Easy
SUITABLE GROWING AREA: Windowsill, lights, greenhouse
LIGHT: Low to medium
TEMPERATURE: Intermediate
RECOMMENDED POTTING MEDIUM: Fine-textured, well-drained mix
SPECIAL CULTURAL TIP: Keep the growing medium damp to avoid pleating of the foliage. Make sure potting mix is fresh and not broken down as this plant does not tolerate a soggy medium.

Lycaste Aquila 'Détente' FCC/AOS

PRONUNCIATION: lye-KASS-tee
ORIGIN: *Lycaste* Brugensis × *Lycaste* Jason
DESCRIPTION AND QUALITIES: This hybrid has in its parentage four *Lycaste* species—*Lyc. longipetala*, *Lyc. skinneri*, *Lyc. lasioglossa*, and *Lyc. macrobulbon*.
INTENSITY OF FRAGRANCE: Light
WHEN FRAGRANT: Day
DESCRIPTION OF FRAGRANCE: Sweet floral

FLOWER DESCRIPTION: Peach-colored flowers 4 inches (10 cm) wide. Inflorescence 6 inches (15 cm) tall, with a single flower.
SEASON OF BLOOM: Spring to summer
MATURE PLANT: Reaches 12–18 inches (30–45 cm) tall.
EASE OF CULTURE: Intermediate
SUITABLE GROWING AREA: Windowsill, greenhouse
LIGHT: Medium to high
TEMPERATURE: Intermediate
RECOMMENDED POTTING MEDIUM: Medium-textured epiphytic mix
SPECIAL CULTURAL TIP: Provide a rest period during the winter to induce flowering.

This select clone, *Lycaste* Aquila 'Détente' FCC/AOS, was awarded the American Orchid Society's highest award, the First Class Certificate.

Lycaste Imschootiana

PRONUNCIATION: lye-KASS-tee
ORIGIN: *Lycaste cruenta* × *Lycaste skinneri*
DESCRIPTION AND QUALITIES: A lovely softly colored, lightly scented lycaste.
INTENSITY OF FRAGRANCE: Light
WHEN FRAGRANT: Day
DESCRIPTION OF FRAGRANCE: Spicy
FLOWER DESCRIPTION: Beautiful, well-shaped, white to cream-colored flowers with rose-colored specks, each bloom 4 inches (10 cm) across. Inflorescence 6 inches (15 cm) tall, with a single flower.
SEASON OF BLOOM: Winter
MATURE PLANT: Foliage grows to about 12 inches (30 cm).
EASE OF CULTURE: Intermediate
SUITABLE GROWING AREA: Windowsill, lights, greenhouse
LIGHT: Medium to high
TEMPERATURE: Cool to intermediate
RECOMMENDED POTTING MEDIUM: In a clay pot with a mix of rock wool and perlite or bark and perlite

The delicate creamy flowers and spicy scent make *Lycaste* Imschootiana a favorite. PHOTO BY ALLEN BLACK

SPECIAL CULTURAL TIP: If possible, grow the plant in the cooler area of your growing area. Greatly reduce water from late fall to early winter until buds appear.

Lycaste Lucianii

PRONUNCIATION: lye-KASS-tee
ORIGIN: *Lycaste skinneri* × *Lycaste lasioglossa*
DESCRIPTION AND QUALITIES: A very handsome, hardy, easy-to-grow lycaste.
INTENSITY OF FRAGRANCE: Strong
WHEN FRAGRANT: Day
DESCRIPTION OF FRAGRANCE: Sweet and spicy
FLOWER DESCRIPTION: Rose-pink sepals contrast with much smaller white petals, and a fuzzy red lip with yellow in the throat. Flowers 6 inches (15 cm) across. Inflorescence 6–8 inches (15–20 cm) tall, with a single flower.
SEASON OF BLOOM: Variable
MATURE PLANT: Reaches 12–16 inches (30–45 cm) high.
EASE OF CULTURE: Intermediate
SUITABLE GROWING AREA: Windowsill, greenhouse
LIGHT: Medium
TEMPERATURE: Intermediate
RECOMMENDED POTTING MEDIUM: Medium-textured epiphytic mix

Rosy pink *Lycaste* Lucianii adds a touch of elegance and fragrance to any orchid collection.

Zygopetalum Artur Elle 'Tanzanite' AM/AOS

PRONUNCIATION: zeye-go-PET-a-lum
ORIGIN: *Zygopetalum* Blackii × *Zygopetalum* BG White
DESCRIPTION AND QUALITIES: A tall, dark, and handsome zygopetalum.
INTENSITY OF FRAGRANCE: Strong
WHEN FRAGRANT: Day
DESCRIPTION OF FRAGRANCE: Hyacinth, violets, sweet perfume
FLOWER DESCRIPTION: Green flowers overlaid with maroon. Wide white lip covered with purple. Flowers 2³/₄ inches (7 cm) across.

Zygopetalum Artur Elle 'Tanzanite' AM/AOS fills the room with its hyacinth fragrance.

SEASON OF BLOOM: Spring to summer
MATURE PLANT: Reaches 18 inches (45 cm) tall.
EASE OF CULTURE: Intermediate
SUITABLE GROWING AREA: Windowsill, greenhouse
LIGHT: Medium
TEMPERATURE: Cool to intermediate
RECOMMENDED POTTING MEDIUM: Medium-textured epiphytic mix
OTHER FRAGRANT ZYGOPETALUMS: *Zygopetalum*—sweet; *Z*. BG White
'Stonehurst' HCC/AOS, AM/AOS—hyacinths, violets, sweet perfume;
Z. crinitum—spicy-floral, narcissus; *Z. intermedium*—rose, lilac; *Z. mackayi*—hyacinth, narcissus; *Z. maxillare*—floral; *Z.* Redvale 'Fire Kiss'—
hyacinth.

Paphiopedilum and *Phragmipedium* Species

Paphiopedilum delenatii
PRONUNCIATION: paff-ee-oh-PED-i-lum
AKA: *Cypripedium delenatii*
ORIGIN: Vietnam
DESCRIPTION AND QUALITIES: A form of this species, discovered from Vietnam in the 1990s, is more vigorous and easier growing than the older form, and is the one most often sold today.
INTENSITY OF FRAGRANCE: Light
WHEN FRAGRANT: Day

Paphiopedilum delenatii is one of the few Asian slipper orchids with a fragrance.

DESCRIPTION OF FRAGRANCE: Rose, lemon honey.

FLOWER DESCRIPTION: Pale pink flowers with darker pink pouch. Flowers 3 inches (7.5 cm) across. Inflorescence 8–10 inches (20–25 cm) tall, bearing one to two flowers. SEASON OF BLOOM: Variable

MATURE PLANT: Very compact habit with gorgeous mottled, dark green foliage 4 inches (10 cm) long.

EASE OF CULTURE: Easy

SUITABLE GROWING AREA: Windowsill, lights, greenhouse

LIGHT: Low

TEMPERATURE: Intermediate

RECOMMENDED POTTING MEDIUM: Fine-textured mix

SPECIAL CULTURAL TIP: Easy to grow with other paphiopedilums.

COMMENT: First discovered in northern Vietnam by a French army officer in 1914. Prior to the early 1990s most of the plants of this species available for sale originated from plants raised from seed by the famous French orchid nursery of Messrs. Vacherot and Lecoufle.

Paphiopedilum malipoense

PRONUNCIATION: paff-ee-oh-PED-i-lum

ORIGIN: Southern China, Vietnam

DESCRIPTION AND QUALITIES: A species with various flower forms.

INTENSITY OF FRAGRANCE: Light

WHEN FRAGRANT: Day

DESCRIPTION OF FRAGRANCE: Raspberry, apple

FLOWER DESCRIPTION: Distinctive flower with green petals and sepals. Flowers 3–4 inches (7.5–10 cm) across. Inflorescence tall, at least 12 inches (30 cm), usually bearing one flower.

Slipper orchid *Paphiopedilum malipoense* rewards the grower with an exotic flower and a raspberry scent.

SEASON OF BLOOM: Winter to spring
MATURE PLANT: Leaves beautifully marked and 4–6 inches (10–15 cm) long.
EASE OF CULTURE: Intermediate
SUITABLE GROWING AREA: Windowsill, lights, greenhouse
LIGHT: Low
TEMPERATURE: Intermediate
RECOMMENDED POTTING MEDIUM: Fine-textured mix
COMMENT: First described by notable Chinese botanists Sing-Chi Chen and
Zhan-Huo Tsi in 1984.
OTHER FRAGRANT PAPHIOPEDILUMS: *Paph. emersonii*—chocolate; *Paph.*
Joyce Hasagawa—raspberry; *Paph. kolopakingii*—honeysuckle; *Paph.*
Lynleigh Koopowitz—raspberry.

Phragmipedium Wilcox AM/AOS

PRONUNCIATION: frag-mi-PEE-dee-um
AKA: *Cypripedium schlimii*
ORIGIN: *Phragmipedium schlimii* × *Phragmipedium* Sedenii
DESCRIPTION AND QUALITIES: A well-grown, mature species of this orchid
can be in bloom most of the year.
INTENSITY OF FRAGRANCE: Light
WHEN FRAGRANT: Day
DESCRIPTION OF FRAGRANCE: Rose
FLOWER DESCRIPTION: White flowers with pink pouches borne successively
along the inflorescence. Flowers 2 inches (5 cm) wide. Inflorescence up
to 12 inches (30 cm) tall, bearing two or three flowers.

Phragmipedium Wilcox AM/AOS is one of the few scented
phragmipediums.

SEASON OF BLOOM: Spring
MATURE PLANT: Reaches up to 18 inches (45 cm) tall but frequently smaller.
EASE OF CULTURE: Intermediate
SUITABLE GROWING AREA: Windowsill, greenhouse
LIGHT: Low to medium
TEMPERATURE: Intermediate
RECOMMENDED POTTING MEDIUM: Light, well-drained mix
SPECIAL CULTURAL TIP: Keep growing medium damp.
COMMENT: Discovered by L. J. Schlim in 1852.

Other Orchid Hybrids

Paphiopedilum Armeni White

PRONUNCIATION: paff-ee-oh-PED-i-lum
ORIGIN: *Paphiopedilum armeniacum* × *Paphiopedilum delenatii*
FRAGRANT PARENTS: *Paphiopedilum delenatii*
DESCRIPTION AND QUALITIES: A vigorous plant with beautifully marked foliage and elegant flowers.
INTENSITY OF FRAGRANCE: Light
WHEN FRAGRANT: Day
DESCRIPTION OF FRAGRANCE: Citrus
FLOWER DESCRIPTION: Creamy white flowers $3^{1}/_{2}$ inches (9 cm) wide. Inflorescence about 18 inches (45 cm) long, with one or two flowers.
SEASON OF BLOOM: Spring to summer
MATURE PLANT: A compact plant 6 inches (15 cm) high and 8–10 inches (20–25 cm) wide. Foliage a very attractive dark patterned green.
EASE OF CULTURE: Easy
SUITABLE GROWING AREA: Windowsill, lights, greenhouse
LIGHT: Low
TEMPERATURE: Intermediate
RECOMMENDED POTTING MEDIUM: Fine- to medium-textured orchid mix

The soft white flowers of slipper orchid *Paphiopedilum* Armeni White emit a delicate citrus fragrance.

The Pleurothallid Alliance Hybrids

Polystachya Darling Star

PRONUNCIATION: pol-lee-STACK-ya

ORIGIN: *Polystachya ottoniana* × *Polystachya virginea*

DESCRIPTION AND QUALITIES: One of the relatively few hybrids found in this genus of miniature plants, Darling Star delivers sweet smelling snowy white, waxy flowers in a compact package.

INTENSITY OF FRAGRANCE: Light

WHEN FRAGRANT: Day

DESCRIPTION OF FRAGRANCE: Floral

FLOWER DESCRIPTION: Clear white flowers borne upside down. Flowers $^3/_4$ inch (2 cm) wide. Inflorescence 3–4 inches (7.5–10 cm) tall, bearing three to four flowers.

SEASON OF BLOOM: Spring

MATURE PLANT: A dwarf grower, about 6 inches (15 cm) high.

EASE OF CULTURE: Intermediate

SUITABLE GROWING AREA: Windowsill, lights, greenhouse

LIGHT: Medium

TEMPERATURE: Intermediate

RECOMMENDED POTTING MEDIUM: Fine-textured mix

Polystachya Darling Star, a miniature gem from J & L Orchids in Connecticut, has crystalline white flowers that shimmer.

OTHER FRAGRANT POLYSTACHYAS: *Pol. bella*—fruity, "like Lemon Pledge"; *Pol. campyloglossa*—bananas, strawberries; *Pol. cultriformis*—lily-of-the valley, lime blossoms; *Pol. fallax*—jasmine, tropical fruit; *Pol. mazumbaiensis*—rose, gardenia; *Pol. pubescens*—honey.

"Stinkers"

Bulbophyllum echinolabium
PRONUNCIATION: bulb-oh-FILL-um
ORIGIN: Borneo, Sulawesi
DESCRIPTION AND QUALITIES: A star among the bulbophyllums because of its large striking flower.
INTENSITY OF FRAGRANCE: Strong
WHEN FRAGRANT: Day
DESCRIPTION OF FRAGRANCE: Carrion

Stinker *Bulbophyllum echinolabium* puts on quite a show, which makes it a conversation piece when it blooms.

FLOWER DESCRIPTION: Dark cream-colored flowers with mahogany stripes. Dramatic for their size, 12 inches (30 cm) long or longer, which makes them among the largest flowers in the genus. Inflorescence 12 inches (30 cm) tall, bearing one flower.
SEASON OF BLOOM: Variable
MATURE PLANT: Compact plant, 6–8 inches (10–15 cm) tall.
EASE OF CULTURE: Intermediate
SUITABLE GROWING AREA: Windowsill, lights, greenhouse
LIGHT: Low to medium
TEMPERATURE: Intermediate to warm
RECOMMENDED POTTING MEDIUM: Medium-textured, well-drained mix, tree fern, or bark

Bulbophyllum phalaenopsis
PRONUNCIATION: bulb-oh-FILL-um
AKA: *Bulbophyllum giganteum*
ORIGIN: New Guinea
DESCRIPTION AND QUALITIES: *Bulbophyllum* species with dark flower colors are frequently "stinkers."
INTENSITY OF FRAGRANCE: Strong

WHEN FRAGRANT: Day

DESCRIPTION OF FRAGRANCE: Carrion

FLOWER DESCRIPTION: Dark red flowers with yellow protuberances that according to Emly Siegerist (2001, p. 127) make them look "(at least to flies) [like] rotting flesh covered with maggots." Flowers 1½ inches (4 cm) across. Inflorescence 8–10 inches (20–25 cm), bearing many flowers.

SEASON OF BLOOM: Variable

MATURE PLANT: Very large leaves, resembling *Phalaenopsis gigantea*.

EASE OF CULTURE: Intermediate

SUITABLE GROWING AREA: Windowsill, lights, greenhouse

LIGHT: Low to medium

TEMPERATURE: Intermediate

RECOMMENDED POTTING MEDIUM: Mounted because of its long pendulous leaves

COMMENT: A huge specimen of this plant with leaves about 4 feet (1.2 meters) long was awarded a Certificate of Cultural Merit at the 2004 New York International Orchid Show. It was said to be valued at about $10,000!

OTHER FRAGRANT BULBOPHYLLUMS: *Bulb. beccarii*—said to smell like 100 dead elephants rotting in the sun.

Bulbophyllum phalaenopsis can empty a whole room of people with its foul odor when it is in full bloom.

Oncidium crispum

PRONUNCIATION: on-SID-ee-um

ORIGIN: Brazil

DESCRIPTION AND QUALITIES: The brown flowers with yellow markings make this orchid a favorite with floral artists.

The flower of *Oncidium crispum* is quite attractive, but its musty scent is not one of its assets.

INTENSITY OF FRAGRANCE: Light

WHEN FRAGRANT: Day

DESCRIPTION OF FRAGRANCE: Musty, like cockroaches

FLOWER DESCRIPTION: Rust-red flowers and lip, with yellow and orange markings on the lip. Flowers 3 inches (8 cm) across. Inflorescence long up to 3 feet (90 cm) long, bearing up to 40 to 80 flowers.

SEASON OF BLOOM: Spring to summer

MATURE PLANT: Leaves 6–8 inches (15–20 cm) tall.

EASE OF CULTURE: Intermediate

SUITABLE GROWING AREA: Windowsill, greenhouse

LIGHT: Medium to high

TEMPERATURE: Intermediate to warm

RECOMMENDED POTTING MEDIUM: Medium-textured epiphytic mix

COMMENT: Introduced and described by Messrs. Loddiges in 1832.

Appendix A

Orchids by Ease of Culture

Easy Culture

Aerangis biloba
Aerangis citrata
Aerangis fastuosa
Aeranthes Grandiose
Aerides odorata
Angraecum compactum
Angraecum distichum
Angraecum germinyanum
Angraecum leonis
Angraecum White Emblem
Angranthes Grandalena
Arundina graminifolia
Ascofinetia Cherry Blossom
  'Delicado'
Beallara Marfitch 'Howard's Dream'
  AM/AOS
Bothriochilus bellus
Brassavola Little Stars
Brassavola Yaki 'Black's Best'
Brassavola cordata
Brassavola nodosa
Brassavola tuberculata
Brassia gireoudiana
Brassia longissima 'Pumpkin Patch'
Brassia verrucosa

Brassidium Dragon Flight 'Fluff'
Brassocattleya Binosa 'Kirk'
  AM/AOS
Brassocattleya Mt. Hood
Brassolaelia Memoria Bernice
  Foster
Brassolaelia Yellow Bird
Brassolaeliocattleya Momilani
  Rainbow
Bulbophyllum beccarii
Bulbophyllum hamatipes
Bulbophyllum laxiflorum
Bulbophyllum lobbii
Bulbophyllum rothschildianum
Cattleya Chocolate Drop 'Kodama'
  AM/AOS
Cattleya luteola
Cochleanthes Moliere
Cochleanthes discolor
Coelogyne Intermedia
Coelogyne ochracea
Darwinara Charm 'Blue Star'
Dendrobium Chrystaline
Dendrobium Comet King 'Akatsuki'
Dendrobium Sea Mary 'Snow King'

Dendrobium Sweet Song 'Memory'
Dendrobium kingianum
Dendrobium nobile
Dendrobium nobile var. *virginale*
Doritaenopsis Garnet Elf 'Mary'
Doritaenopsis Phoenix Fire 'Cardinal'
Encyclia adenocaula
Encyclia fragrans
Encyclia phoenicea
Encyclia radiata
Epicattleya Dora Tinschert 'Springdale' HCC/AOS
Epidendrum ciliare
Epidendrum phoeniceum
Gongora horichiana
Laelia anceps
Laelia perrinii
Laeliocattleya Angel Love
Laeliocattleya Jungle Festival
Laeliocattleya Mari's Song 'CTM 217' HCC/AOS
Laeliocattleya Mini Purple
Laeliocattleya Nora's Melody
Lycaste aromatica
Lycaste brevispatha
Lycaste cruenta
Lycaste powellii
Maxillaria seymouriana
Maxillaria tenuifolia
Milpasia Leslie Garay
Milpasia Milt's Choice 'Helen of Troy'
Miltoniopsis roezlii
Miltoniopsis santanaei
Neostylis Lou Sneary
Neostylis Lou Sneary 'Blue Moon'
Neostylis Lou Sneary 'Pinky' AM/AOS
Odontioda Vesta 'Charm'
Oncidium Issaku Nagata 'Volcano Queen' HCC/AOS
Oncidium Gold Dust

Oncidium Sharry Baby
Oncidium Sharry Baby 'Misaki'
Oncidium Tsiku Marguerite
Oncidium Twinkle 'Fragrance Fantasy'
Oncidium Twinkle 'Red Fantasy'
Oncidium cheirophorum
Oncidium longipes
Oncidium maculatum
Oncidium ornithorhynchum 'Lilac Blossom'
Paphiopedilum Armeni White
Paphiopedilum delenatii
Phalaenopsis Caribbean Sunset 'Sweet Fragrance'
Phalaenopsis Desert Red 'Ruby'
Phalaenopsis Dotty Woodson 'Claudette' HCC/AOS
Phalaenopsis Ember 'Blumen Insel' AM/AOS
Phalaenopsis Mary Lillian Taylor 'Desert Orange' AM/AOS
Phalaenopsis Mini Mark
Phalaenopsis Orchid World 'Bonnie Vasquez' AM/AOS
Phalaenopsis Orchid World 'Roman Holiday' AM/AOS
Phalaenopsis Perfection Is 'Chen' FCC/AOS
Phalaenopsis Samba
Phalaenopsis Sweet Memory 'Amy Dawn' AM/AOS
Phalaenopsis Valentinii
Phalaenopsis Wes Addison 'Blood Brother'
Phalaenopsis schilleriana
Polystachya bella
Potinara Burana Beauty 'Burana' HCC/AOS
Potinara Free Spirit 'Lea' AM/AOS
Sigmatostalix radicans 'HMO's Petite Prince'

Spathoglottis deplanche
Stanhopea oculata
Trichopilia suavis

Tuberolabium kotoense
Tuberolabium odoratissium

Intermediate Culture

Acampe papillosa
Acineta superba
Aerangis appendiculata
Aerangis articulata
Aerangis brachycarpa
Aerangis confusa
Aerangis kirkii
Aerangis kotschyana
Aerangis modesta
Aerangis mooreana
Aerangis mystacidii
Aerangis somalensis
Aerides crassifolia
Aerides falcata
Aerides falcata var. houlletiana
Aerides fieldingii
Aerides quinquevulnera
Amesiella philippinense
Angraecum Lemforde White Beauty
Angraecum Veitchii
Angraecum aporoides
Angraecum birrinense
Angraecum boisserianum
Angraecum bosseri
Angraecum didieri
Angraecum eburneum
Angraecum eichlerianum
Angraecum magdalenae
Angraecum sesquipedale
Anguloa clowesii
Ansellia africana
Bifrenaria harrisoniae
Brassavola cucullata
Brassavola flagellaris
Brassavola martiana
Brassia ochroleuca

Brassolaelia Sarah Black
Brassolaeliocattleya Arthur Bossin
    'Rapture'
Brassolaeliocattleya Formosan Gold
Brassolaeliocattleya George King
    'Serendipity' AM/AOS
Brassolaeliocattleya Goldenzelle
    'Lemon Chiffon' AM/AOS
Brassolaeliocattleya Haw Yuan
    Beauty 'Orchis'
Brassolaeliocattleya Hawaiian
    Avalanche
Brassolaeliocattleya Pamela Hether-
    ington 'Coronation' FCC/AOS
Brassolaeliocattleya Ports of Paradise
    'Emerald Isle' HCC/AOS
Brassolaeliocattleya Rio's Green
    Magic
Bulbophyllum ambrosia
Bulbophyllum cocoinum
Bulbophyllum comosum
Bulbophyllum echinolabium
Bulbophyllum maximum
Bulbophyllum odoratissimum
Bulbophyllum phalaenopsis
Bulbophyllum suavissimum
Cadetia chionantha
Cadetia taylori
Catasetum Orchidglade 'Davie
    Ranches' AM/AOS
Catasetum candida
Catasetum collare
Catasetum discolor
Catasetum expansum
Catasetum fimbriatum
Catasetum gnomus

Catasetum integerrimum
Catasetum maculatum
Catasetum roseum
Catasetum tenebrosum
Catasetum warscewiczii
Cattleya Brabantiae
Cattleya Fascelis
Cattleya Peckhaviensis
Cattleya Pradit Spot 'Black Prince'
Cattleya bicolor var. *grossii*
Cattleya dowiana
Cattleya forbesii
Cattleya granulosa
Cattleya guttata
Cattleya harrisoniana
Cattleya intermedia
Cattleya intermedia 'Carlos'
Cattleya labiata
Cattleya loddigesii
Cattleya lueddemanniana 'Waterfield'
Cattleya maxima 'Mountainside'
Cattleya mossiae
Cattleya quadicolor
Cattleya schilleriana
Cattleya schroederae
Cattleya walkeriana var. *alba*
Cattleya warneri
Cattleya warscewiczii
Caularthron bicornutum
Cirrhopetalum graveolens
Cirrhopetalum ornatissimum
Cochleanthes amazonica
Coelogyne cristata
Coelogyne fimbriata
Coelogyne lawrenceana
Coelogyne pandurata
Coelogyne zurowetzii
Coryanthes bruckmuelleri
Coryanthes leucocorys
Cycnoches chlorochilon
Cycnoches loddigesii
Cycnoches ventricosum

Cycnoches warscewiczii
Cymbidium Golden Elf 'Sundust' HCC/AOS
Cymbidium cyperifolium
Cymbidium eburneum
Cymbidium ensifolium
Cymbidium goeringii
Cymbidium kanran
Cymbidium mastersii
Cymbidium sinensis
Cymbidium suave
Cymbidium tracyanum
Cymbidium virescens
Dendrobium Gai Quest
Dendrobium Jesmond Fancy
Dendrobium Jesmond Gem
Dendrobium Light River
Dendrobium Spring Bride
Dendrobium Spring Doll
Dendrobium anosmum
Dendrobium antennatum
Dendrobium aureum
Dendrobium bellatulum
Dendrobium cariniferum
Dendrobium chrysotoxum
Dendrobium delicatum 'Brechts'
Dendrobium densiflorum
Dendrobium draconis
Dendrobium fimbriatum var. *oculatum*
Dendrobium griffithianum
Dendrobium hainanense
Dendrobium heterocarpum
Dendrobium jenkinsii
Dendrobium lawesii
Dendrobium loddigesii
Dendrobium macrophyllum
Dendrobium moniliforme
Dendrobium monophyllum
Dendrobium musciferum
Dendrobium parishii
Dendrobium primulinum var. *giganteum*

Dendrobium pugioniforme
Dendrobium rhodopterygium var.
  semialba
Dendrobium speciosum
Dendrobium unicum
Dendrobium virgineum
Dendrobium wardianum
Dendrobium williamsonii
Dendrochilum cobbianum
Dendrochilum glumaceum
Dendrochilum arachnites
Dendrochilum magnum
Diaphananthe pellucida
Diaphananthe pulchella
Dracula chestertonii
Encyclia cordigera
Encyclia lancifolia
Encyclia polybulbon
Encyclia tampensis
Encyclia trulla
Epidendrum difforme
Epidendrum falcatum
Epidendrum inversum
Epidendrum nocturnum
Epidendrum parkinsonianum
Epilaelia Beverly Shea
Eria gigantea 'Waterfield'
Eria hyacinthoides
Eurychone rothschildianum
Gongora galeata
Gongora grossa
Gongora leucochila
Gongora pleiochroma
Gongora quinquenervis
Gongora unicolor
Haraella odorata
Iwanagaara Appleblossom 'Fantastic'
Jumellea confusa
Jumellea densifoliata
Jumellea sagittata
Laelia albida
Laelia lundii

Laelia pumila var. *coerulea*
Laelia purpurata var. *werckhauseri*
Laelia rubescens
Laeliocattleya Angel Love
Laeliocattleya Hausermann's Sultan
Laeliocattleya Whitiniae
Leptotes bicolor
Leptotes unicolor
Lycaste Alan Salzman
Lycaste Aquila 'Détente' FCC/AOS
Lycaste Imschootiana
Lycaste Lucianii
Lycaste Walnut Valley 'Black's Glow'
Lycaste bradeorum
Lycaste ciliata
Lycaste cochleata
Lycaste deppei
Lycaste lanipes
Lycaste leucantha
Lycaste locusta
Masdevallia Confetti
Masdevallia agaster
Masdevallia attenuata
Masdevallia cyclotega
Masdevallia glandulosa
Masdevallia laucheana
Masdevallia livingstoneana
Masdevallia mejiana
Masdevallia triangularis
Maxillaria ochroleuca
Maxillaria picta
Maxillaria rufescens
Maxillaria sanderiana
Meiracyllium trinasutum
Miltonia regnellii
Miltonia schroederiana
Miltonia spectabilis
Miltonia spectabilis var. *moreliana*
Miltoniopsis Bert Field
Miltoniopsis Celle 'Wasserfall'
  AM/AOS
Miltoniopsis Hajime Ono

Miltoniopsis Hamburg 'Red Velvet'
Miltoniopsis phalaenopsis
Neofinetia falcata
Odontobrassia Fangtastic Bob
  Henley
Odontocidium Tiger Crow 'Golden
  Girl' HCC/AOS
Odontoglossum pendulum
Odontoglossum pulchellum
Oeniella polystachys
Oncidium concolor
Oncidium crispum
Oncidium cucullatum
Oncidium microchilum
Oncidium tigrinum
Otaara Haw Yuan Bay 'She Shu'
Paphiopedilum Joyce Hasagawa
Paphiopedilum Lynleigh Koopowitz
Paphiopedilum emersonii
Paphiopedilum kolopakingii
Paphiopedilum malipoense
Peristeria elata
Phalaenopsis Kilby Cassviola 'Sweet
  Fragrance'
Phalaenopsis amboinensis
Phalaenopsis bellina
Phalaenopsis fasciata
Phalaenopsis gigantea
Phalaenopsis hieroglyphica
Phalaenopsis lueddemanniana
Phalaenopsis mannii
Phalaenopsis modesta
Phalaenopsis violacea
Phragmipedium Wilcox AM/AOS
Pleurothallis cocornaensis
Pleurothallis ramulosa
Polystachya Darling Star
Polystachya campyloglossa
Polystachya cultriformis
Polystachya fallax
Polystachya mazumbaiensis
Polystachya pubescens

Potinara Twentyfour Carat 'Lea'
  AM/AOS
Rangaeris amaniensis
Rhyncholaelia glauca
Rhynchostylis coelestis
Rhynchostylis gigantea
Rhynchostylis gigantea Sagarik Strain
Rhynchostylis gigantea var. *alba*
Rhynchostylis illustre
Rhynchostylis retusa
Ronnyara Manuel Ugarte 'H & R'
Schoenorchis fragrans
Schoenorchis gemmata
Sedirea japonica
Sobennikoffia humbertiana
Sophrolaeliocattleya Haw Yuan Star
  'Pink Lady'
Stanhopea candida
Stanhopea cirrhata
Stanhopea costaricensis
Stanhopea ecornuta
Stanhopea embreei
Stanhopea grandiflora
Stanhopea jenischiana
Stanhopea pulla
Stanhopea reichenbachiana
Stanhopea saccata
Stanhopea tigrina
Stanhopea tricornis
Stanhopea wardii
Stelis pusilla
Thunia marshalliana
Trichocentrum albococcineum
Trichocentrum Nathakhun
Trichocentrum tigrinum
Trichoglottis philippinensis 'Pololei'
Trichoglottis wenzellii
Trichopilia fragrans
Vanda Pat Delight
Vanda coerulescens
Vanda cristata
Vanda dearei

Vanda denisoniana
Vanda roeblingiana
Vanda tesselata
Vanda tricolor
Vanda tricolor var. *suavis*
Vascostylis Crownfox Red Gem
Vascostylis Tham Yuen Hae 'Blue Queen' HCC/RSPC, JC/AOS, HCC/AOS
Woodwardara Adelaide
Zygoneria

Zygopetalum
Zygopetalum Artur Elle 'Tanzanite' AM/AOS
Zygopetalum BG White 'Stonehurst' HCC/AOS, AM/AOS
Zygopetalum Redvale 'Fire Kiss'
Zygopetalum crinitum
Zygopetalum intermedium
Zygopetalum mackayi
Zygopetalum maxillare

Challenging Culture

Aerides lawrenceae
Aerides lawrenceae var. *sanderiana*
Angraecum Longiscott 'Lea'
Cattleya aclandiae

Encyclia citrina
Laelia tenebrosa
Rhyncholaelia digbyana
Zygocolax

Appendix B

Orchids by Light Requirements

Low Light (less than 1500 footcandles)

Doritaenopsis Garnet Elf 'Mary'
Doritaenopsis Phoenix Fire 'Cardinal'
Paphiopedilum Armeni White
Paphiopedilum Joyce Hasagawa
Paphiopedilum Lynleigh Koopowitz
Paphiopedilum delenatii
Paphiopedilum emersonii
Paphiopedilum kolopakingii
Paphiopedilum malipoense
Phalaenopsis Caribbean Sunset 'Sweet Fragrance'
Phalaenopsis Desert Red 'Ruby'
Phalaenopsis Dotty Woodson 'Claudette' HCC/AOS
Phalaenopsis Ember 'Blumen Insel' AM/AOS
Phalaenopsis Kilby Cassviola 'Sweet Fragrance'
Phalaenopsis Mary Lillian Taylor 'Desert Orange' AM/AOS
Phalaenopsis Perfection Is 'Chen' FCC/AOS
Phalaenopsis Samba
Phalaenopsis Sweet Memory 'Amy Dawn' AM/AOS
Phalaenopsis Valentinii
Phalaenopsis Wes Addison 'Blood Brother'
Phalaenopsis amboinensis
Phalaenopsis bellina
Phalaenopsis fasciata
Phalaenopsis hieroglyphica
Phalaenopsis lueddemanniana
Phalaenopsis mannii
Phalaenopsis modesta
Phalaenopsis schilleriana

Low to Medium Light

Angraecum compactum
Bothriochilus bellus
Bulbophyllum beccarii
Bulbophyllum cocoinum
Bulbophyllum comosum
Bulbophyllum echinolabium
Bulbophyllum hamatipes
Bulbophyllum laxiflorum
Bulbophyllum odoratissimum
Bulbophyllum phalaenopsis

Bulbophyllum suavissimum
Cattleya lueddemanniana
  'Waterfield'
Cirrhopetalum graveolens
Cirrhopetalum ornatissimum
Cochleanthes Moliere
Cochleanthes amazonica
Cochleanthes discolor
Dracula chestertonii
Eurychone rothschildianum
Masdevallia Confetti
Masdevallia agaster
Masdevallia attenuata
Masdevallia glandulosa
Masdevallia mejiana

Masdevallia triangularis
Miltonia regnellii
Miltoniopsis Bert Field
Miltoniopsis Hajime Ono
Miltoniopsis santanaei
Odontioda Vesta 'Charm'
Phalaenopsis Mini Mark
Phalaenopsis Orchid World 'Roman
  Holiday' AM/AOS
Phalaenopsis gigantea
Phalaenopsis violacea
Phragmipedium Wilcox AM/AOS
Pleurothallis cocornaensis
Spathoglottis deplanche

Medium Light (1500–2500 footcandles)

Aerangis appendiculata
Aerangis articulata
Aerangis biloba
Aerangis brachycarpa
Aerangis citrata
Aerangis confusa
Aerangis fastuosa
Aerangis kirkii
Aerangis kotschyana
Aerangis modesta
Aerangis mooreana
Aerangis mystacidii
Aerangis somalensis
Aeranthes Grandiose
Aerides crassifolia
Aerides fieldingii
Amesiella philippinense
Angraecum didieri
Angraecum distichum
Angraecum germinyanum
Angraecum leonis
Angraecum magdalenae
Angranthes Grandalena
Anguloa clowesii

Ascofinetia Cherry Blossom
  'Delicado'
Beallara Marfitch 'Howard's Dream'
  AM/AOS
Bifrenaria harrisoniae
Brassavola cordata
Brassidium Dragon Flight 'Fluff'
Brassolaeliocattleya Arthur Bossin
  'Rapture'
Brassolaeliocattleya Momilani
  Rainbow
Bulbophyllum ambrosia
Bulbophyllum lobbii
Bulbophyllum maximum
Bulbophyllum rothschildianum
Cadetia chionantha
Cadetia taylori
Catasetum Orchidglade 'Davie
  Ranches' AM/AOS
Catasetum candida
Catasetum collare
Catasetum discolor
Catasetum expansum
Catasetum fimbriatum

Catasetum gnomus
Catasetum integerrimum
Catasetum roseum
Catasetum warscewiczii
Cattleya Chocolate Drop 'Kodama' AM/AOS
Cattleya Peckhaviensis
Cattleya Pradit Spot 'Black Prince'
Cattleya loddigesii
Caularthron bicornutum
Coelogyne fimbriata
Coelogyne lawrenceana
Coelogyne ochracea
Coryanthes bruckmuelleri
Coryanthes leucocorys
Cycnoches chlorochilon
Cycnoches loddigesii
Cycnoches ventricosum
Cycnoches warscewiczii
Darwinara Charm 'Blue Star'
Dendrobium Chrystaline
Dendrochilum glumaceum
Dendrochilum arachnites
Dendrochilum magnum
Diaphananthe pellucida
Diaphananthe pulchella
Encyclia adenocaula
Encyclia citrina
Encyclia fragrans
Encyclia lancifolia
Encyclia phoenicea
Encyclia polybulbon
Encyclia tampensis
Encyclia trulla
Epicattleya Dora Tinschert 'Springdale' HCC/AOS
Epidendrum ciliare
Epidendrum difforme
Epidendrum falcatum
Epidendrum parkinsonianum
Epidendrum phoeniceum

Eria gigantea 'Waterfield'
Eria hyacinthoides
Gongora galeata
Gongora grossa
Gongora horichiana
Gongora leucochila
Gongora pleiochroma
Gongora quinquenervis
Gongora unicolor
Haraella odorata
Jumellea confusa
Jumellea densifoliata
Jumellea sagittata
Laeliocattleya Angel Love
Laeliocattleya Jungle Festival
Laeliocattleya Mini Purple
Laeliocattleya Nora's Melody
Laeliocattleya Whitiniae
Leptotes bicolor
Leptotes unicolor
Lycaste Alan Salzman
Lycaste Lucianii
Lycaste brevispatha
Lycaste cochleata
Lycaste cruenta
Lycaste locusta
Lycaste powellii
Masdevallia cyclotega
Masdevallia laucheana
Masdevallia livingstoneana
Maxillaria ochroleuca
Maxillaria picta
Maxillaria rufescens
Maxillaria sanderiana
Maxillaria seymouriana
Maxillaria tenuifolia
Meiracyllium trinasutum
Milpasia Leslie Garay
Milpasia Milt's Choice 'Helen of Troy'
Miltonia schroederiana

Miltonia spectabilis
Miltonia spectabilis var. *moreliana*
Miltoniopsis Celle 'Wasserfall'
    AM/AOS
Miltoniopsis Hamburg 'Red Velvet'
Miltoniopsis phalaenopsis
Miltoniopsis roezlii
Neofinetia falcata
Neostylis Lou Sneary
Neostylis Lou Sneary 'Blue Moon'
Neostylis Lou Sneary 'Pinky' AM/AOS
Odontobrassia Fangtastic Bob Henley
Odontocidium Tiger Crow 'Golden
    Girl' HCC/AOS
Odontoglossum pendulum
Odontoglossum pulchellum
Oeniella polystachys
Oncidium longipes
Oncidium Gold Dust
Oncidium Issaku Nagata 'Volcano
    Queen' HCC/AOS
Oncidium Sharry Baby
Oncidium Sharry Baby 'Misaki'
Oncidium Tsiku Marguerite
Oncidium Twinkle 'Fragrance Fan-
    tasy'
Oncidium Twinkle 'Red Fantasy'
Oncidium cheirophorum
Oncidium concolor
Oncidium cucullatum
Oncidium maculatum
Oncidium microchilum
Oncidium ornithorhynchum 'Lilac
    Blossom'
Oncidium tigrinum
Peristeria elata
Phalaenopsis Orchid World 'Bonnie
    Vasquez' AM/AOS
Pleurothallis ramulosa
Polystachya Darling Star
Polystachya bella

Polystachya campyloglossa
Polystachya cultriformis
Polystachya fallax
Polystachya mazumbaiensis
Polystachya pubescens
Potinara Burana Beauty 'Burana'
    HCC/AOS
Potinara Twentyfour Carat 'Lea'
    AM/AOS
Rhyncholaelia glauca
Rhynchostylis coelestis
Rhynchostylis gigantea
Rhynchostylis gigantea Sagarik Strain
Rhynchostylis gigantea var. *alba*
Rhynchostylis illustre
Rhynchostylis retusa
Schoenorchis fragrans
Schoenorchis gemmata
Sedirea japonica
Sigmatostalix radicans 'HMO's Petite
    Prince'
Sobennikoffia humbertiana
Stanhopea candida
Stanhopea cirrhata
Stanhopea costaricensis
Stanhopea embreei
Stanhopea grandiflora
Stanhopea jenischiana
Stanhopea oculata
Stanhopea pulla
Stanhopea reichenbachiana
Stanhopea saccata
Stanhopea tigrina
Stanhopea tricornis
Stanhopea wardii
Stelis pusilla
Thunia marshalliana
Trichocentrum albococcineum
Trichoglottis philippinensis 'Pololei'
Trichoglottis wenzellii
Trichopilia fragrans

Trichopilia suavis
Tuberolabium kotoense
Tuberolabium odoratissium
Vascostylis Crownfox Red Gem
Vascostylis Tham Yuen Hae 'Blue Queen' HCC/RSPC, JC/AOS, HCC/AOS
Zygocolax

Zygopetalum Artur Elle 'Tanzanite' AM/AOS
Zygopetalum BG White 'Stonehurst' HCC/AOS, AM/AOS
Zygopetalum Redvale 'Fire Kiss'
Zygopetalum intermedium
Zygopetalum mackayi
Zygopetalum maxillare

Medium to High Light

Acampe papillosa
Acineta superba
Aerides falcata
Aerides falcata var. *houlletiana*
Aerides lawrenceae
Aerides lawrenceae var. *sanderiana*
Aerides odorata
Aerides quinquevulnera
Angraecum aporoides
Angraecum birrinense
Angraecum bosseri
Angraecum boisserianum
Angraecum eburneum
Angraecum eichlerianum
Angraecum Lemforde White Beauty
Angraecum Longiscott 'Lea'
Angraecum sesquipedale
Angraecum White Emblem
Brassavola Yaki 'Black's Best'
Brassavola cucullata
Brassavola martiana
Brassavola nodosa
Brassavola tuberculata
Brassia gireoudiana
Brassia longissima 'Pumpkin Patch'
Brassia ochroleuca
Brassia verrucosa
Brassocattleya Binosa 'Kirk' AM/AOS
Brassocattleya Mt. Hood

Brassolaelia Memoria Bernice Foster
Brassolaelia Yellow Bird
Brassolaeliocattleya Formosan Gold
Brassolaeliocattleya George King 'Serendipity' AM/AOS
Brassolaeliocattleya Goldenzelle 'Lemon Chiffon' AM/AOS
Brassolaeliocattleya Haw Yuan Beauty 'Orchis'
Brassolaeliocattleya Hawaiian Avalanche
Brassolaeliocattleya Pamela Hetherington 'Coronation' FCC/AOS
Brassolaeliocattleya Ports of Paradise 'Emerald Isle' HCC/AOS
Brassolaeliocattleya Rio's Green Magic
Catasetum maculatum
Catasetum tenebrosum
Cattleya Brabantiae
Cattleya Fascelis
Cattleya bicolor var. *grossii*
Cattleya dowiana
Cattleya granulosa
Cattleya guttata
Cattleya harrisoniana
Cattleya intermedia
Cattleya intermedia 'Carlos'
Cattleya labiata
Cattleya luteola

Cattleya maxima 'Mountainside'
Cattleya mossiae
Cattleya quadicolor
Cattleya schilleriana
Cattleya schroederae
Cattleya walkeriana var. alba
Cattleya warneri
Cattleya warscewiczii
Coelogyne Intermedia
Coelogyne cristata
Coelogyne pandurata
Coelogyne zurowetzii
Cymbidium ensifolium
Cymbidium mastersii
Cymbidium sinensis
Cymbidium suave
Cymbidium tracyanum
Cymbidium virescens
Dendrobium Comet King 'Akatsuki'
Dendrobium Gai Quest
Dendrobium Jesmond Fancy
Dendrobium Jesmond Gem
Dendrobium Light River
Dendrobium Sea Mary 'Snow King'
Dendrobium Spring Bride
Dendrobium Spring Doll
Dendrobium Sweet Song 'Memory'
Dendrobium anosmum
Dendrobium antennatum
Dendrobium aureum
Dendrobium bellatulum
Dendrobium cariniferum
Dendrobium chrysotoxum
Dendrobium delicatum 'Brechts'
Dendrobium densiflorum
Dendrobium draconis
Dendrobium fimbriatum var.
   oculatum
Dendrobium griffithianum
Dendrobium hainanense
Dendrobium heterocarpum
Dendrobium jenkinsii

Dendrobium kingianum
Dendrobium lawesii
Dendrobium loddigesii
Dendrobium macrophyllum
Dendrobium moniliforme
Dendrobium monophyllum
Dendrobium musciferum
Dendrobium nobile
Dendrobium nobile var. virginale
Dendrobium parishii
Dendrobium primulinum var. gigan-
   teum
Dendrobium pugioniforme
Dendrobium rhodopterygium var.
   semialba
Dendrobium speciosum
Dendrobium unicum
Dendrobium virgineum
Dendrobium wardianum
Dendrobium williamsonii
Dendrochilum cobbianum
Encyclia cordigera
Encyclia radiata
Epidendrum inversum
Epidendrum nocturnum
Epilaelia Beverly Shea
Iwanagaara Appleblossom
   'Fantastic'
Laelia albida
Laelia anceps
Laelia perrinii
Laelia pumila var. coerulea
Laelia purpurata var. werckhauseri
Laelia tenebrosa
Laeliocattleya Hausermann's Sultan
Laeliocattleya Mari's Song 'CTM 217'
   HCC/AOS
Lycaste Aquila 'Détente' FCC/AOS
Lycaste Imschootiana
Lycaste Walnut Valley 'Black's Glow'
Lycaste aromatica
Lycaste bradeorum

Lycaste ciliata
Lycaste deppei
Lycaste lanipes
Lycaste leucantha
Oncidium crispum
Otaara Haw Yuan Bay 'She Shu'
Potinara Free Spirit 'Lea' AM/AOS
Rangaeris amaniensis
Rhyncholaelia digbyana
Ronnyara Manuel Ugarte 'H & R'
Sophrolaeliocattleya Haw Yuan Star
   'Pink Lady'

Stanhopea costaricensis
Stanhopea ecornuta
Trichocentrum Nathakhun
Trichocentrum tigrinum
Vanda Pat Delight
Vanda dearei
Vanda denisoniana
Vanda tesselata
Woodwardara Adelaide
Zygoneria
Zygopetalum crinitum

High Light (2500 footcandles or higher)

Angraecum Veitchii
Ansellia africana
Arundina graminifolia
Brassavola Little Stars
Brassavola flagellaris
Brassolaelia Sarah Black
Cattleya aclandiae
Cattleya forbesii
Cymbidium Golden Elf 'Sundust'
   HCC/AOS
Cymbidium cyperifolium

Cymbidium eburneum
Cymbidium goeringii
Cymbidium kanran
Laelia lundii
Laelia rubescens
Vanda coerulescens
Vanda cristata
Vanda roeblingiana
Vanda tricolor
Vanda tricolor var. *suavis*

Appendix C

Orchids by Nighttime Temperature Preferences

It is assumed that day temperatures will be 15 degrees Fahrenheit (8 degrees Celsius) or warmer than the nighttime temperatures cited here.

Cool Temperature (45–50°F/7–10°C)

Coelogyne ochracea
Cymbidium cyperifolium
Cymbidium eburneum
Cymbidium goeringii
Cymbidium kanran
Cymbidium mastersii
Cymbidium sinensis
Cymbidium suave
Cymbidium tracyanum
Cymbidium virescens
Dendrobium Gai Quest

Cool to Intermediate Temperature

Cadetia chionantha
Cymbidium ensifolium
Dendrobium Chrystaline
Dendrobium Jesmond Fancy
Dendrobium Jesmond Gem
Dendrobium Light River
Dendrobium bellatulum
Dendrobium hainanense
Dendrobium kingianum
Dendrobium primulinum var. *gigan-teum*
Encyclia citrina
Eria hyacinthoides
Lycaste Imschootiana
Lycaste Walnut Valley 'Black's Glow'
Lycaste aromatica
Lycaste bradeorum
Lycaste locusta
Masdevallia Confetti
Masdevallia agaster
Masdevallia attenuata
Masdevallia cyclotega
Masdevallia glandulosa
Masdevallia laucheana
Masdevallia livingstoneana
Masdevallia mejiana
Masdevallia triangularis
Maxillaria sanderiana

Miltoniopsis Bert Field
Miltoniopsis Celle 'Wasserfall'
   AM/AOS
Miltoniopsis Hajime Ono
Miltoniopsis Hamburg 'Red Velvet'
Odontoglossum pulchellum
Thunia marshalliana
Vanda cristata
Zygocolax

Zygopetalum Artur Elle 'Tanzanite'
   AM/AOS
Zygopetalum BG White 'Stonehurst'
   HCC/AOS, AM/AOS
Zygopetalum Redvale 'Fire Kiss'
Zygopetalum crinitum
Zygopetalum intermedium
Zygopetalum mackayi
Zygopetalum maxillare

Intermediate Temperature (55–66°F/12–15°C)

Acampe papillosa
Acineta superba
Aerangis confusa
Aerangis fastuosa
Aerangis kirkii
Aerangis kotschyana
Aerangis somalensis
Angranthes Grandalena
Anguloa clowesii Beallara Marfitch
   'Howard's Dream' AM/AOS
Bifrenaria harrisoniae
Brassia ochroleuca
Brassolaelia Memoria Bernice Foster
Brassolaelia Yellow Bird
Brassolaeliocattleya Arthur Bossin
   'Rapture'
Brassolaeliocattleya Formosan Gold
Brassolaeliocattleya George King
   'Serendipity' AM/AOS
Brassolaeliocattleya Goldenzelle
   'Lemon Chiffon' AM/AOS
Brassolaeliocattleya Haw Yuan
   Beauty 'Orchis'
Brassolaeliocattleya Hawaiian
   Avalanche
Brassolaeliocattleya Momilani
   Rainbow
Brassolaeliocattleya Pamela Hether-
   ington 'Coronation' FCC/AOS

Brassolaeliocattleya Ports of Paradise
   'Emerald Isle' HCC/AOS
Brassolaeliocattleya Rio's Green
   Magic
Bulbophyllum ambrosia
Bulbophyllum beccarii
Bulbophyllum cocoinum
Bulbophyllum maximum
Bulbophyllum phalaenopsis
Bulbophyllum suavissimum
Cadetia taylori
Catasetum Orchidglade 'Davie
   Ranches' AM/AOS
Catasetum candida
Catasetum collare
Catasetum discolor
Catasetum expansum
Catasetum fimbriatum
Catasetum gnomus
Catasetum integerrimum
Catasetum maculatum
Catasetum roseum
Catasetum tenebrosum
Catasetum warscewiczii
Cattleya Brabantiae
Cattleya Chocolate Drop 'Kodama'
   AM/AOS
Cattleya Fascelis
Cattleya Peckhaviensis

Cattleya Pradit Spot 'Black Prince'
Cattleya aclandiae
Cattleya bicolor var. *grossii*
Cattleya dowiana
Cattleya granulosa
Cattleya harrisoniana
Cattleya intermedia
Cattleya intermedia 'Carlos'
Cattleya labiata
Cattleya loddigesii
Cattleya maxima 'Mountainside'
Cattleya mossiae
Cattleya quadicolor
Cattleya schilleriana
Cattleya schroederae
Cattleya walkeriana var. *alba*
Cattleya warneri
Cattleya warscewiczii
Caularthron bicornutum
Cirrhopetalum graveolens
Cirrhopetalum ornatissimum
Cochleanthes Moliere
Cochleanthes amazonica
Cochleanthes discolor
Coelogyne Intermedia
Coelogyne fimbriata
Coelogyne pandurata
Coelogyne zurowetzii
Cycnoches
Cymbidium Golden Elf 'Sundust' HCC/AOS
Darwinara Charm 'Blue Star'
Dendrobium Comet King 'Akatsuki'
Dendrobium Sea Mary 'Snow King'
Dendrobium Spring Bride
Dendrobium Spring Doll
Dendrobium Sweet Song 'Memory'
Dendrobium antennatum
Dendrobium aureum
Dendrobium cariniferum
Dendrobium chrysotoxum

Dendrobium delicatum 'Brechts'
Dendrobium densiflorum
Dendrobium draconis
Dendrobium fimbriatum var. *oculatum*
Dendrobium griffithianum
Dendrobium heterocarpum
Dendrobium jenkinsii
Dendrobium lawesii
Dendrobium macrophyllum
Dendrobium moniliforme
Dendrobium monophyllum
Dendrobium musciferum
Dendrobium nobile
Dendrobium nobile var. *virginale*
Dendrobium parishii
Dendrobium pugioniforme
Dendrobium rhodopterygium var. *semialba*
Dendrobium speciosum
Dendrobium unicum
Dendrobium virgineum
Dendrobium wardianum
Dendrobium williamsonii
Dendrochilum glumaceum
Dendrochilum arachnites
Diaphananthe pellucida
Diaphananthe pulchella
Dracula chestertonii
Encyclia adenocaula
Encyclia fragrans
Encyclia lancifolia
Encyclia phoenicea
Encyclia polybulbon
Encyclia radiata
Encyclia tampensis
Encyclia trulla
Epicattleya Dora Tinschert 'Springdale' HCC/AOS
Epidendrum ciliare
Epidendrum falcatum

Epidendrum inversum
Epidendrum nocturnum
Epidendrum parkinsonianum
Epidendrum phoeniceum
Haraella odorata
Iwanagaara Appleblossom 'Fantastic'
Jumellea confusa
Jumellea densifoliata
Jumellea sagittata
Laelia albida
Laelia anceps
Laelia lundii
Laelia perrinii
Laelia pumila var. *coerulea*
Laelia purpurata var. *werckhauseri*
Laelia rubescens
Laelia tenebrosa
Laeliocattleya Angel Love
Laeliocattleya Hausermann's Sultan
Laeliocattleya Jungle Festival
Laeliocattleya Mari's Song 'CTM 217' HCC/AOS
Laeliocattleya Mini Purple
Laeliocattleya Nora's Melody
Leptotes bicolor
Lycaste Alan Salzman
Lycaste Aquila 'Détente' FCC/AOS
Lycaste Lucianii
Lycaste brevispatha
Lycaste ciliata
Lycaste cochleata
Lycaste cruenta
Lycaste deppei
Lycaste lanipes
Lycaste leucantha
Lycaste powellii
Maxillaria seymouriana
Maxillaria tenuifolia
Meiracyllium trinasutum
Milpasia Leslie Garay
Milpasia Milt's Choice 'Helen of Troy'

Miltonia regnellii
Miltonia schroederiana
Miltonia spectabilis
Miltonia spectabilis var. *moreliana*
Miltoniopsis phalaenopsis
Miltoniopsis roezlii
Miltoniopsis santanaei
Odontioda Vesta 'Charm'
Odontobrassia Fangtastic Bob Henley
Odontocidium Tiger Crow 'Golden Girl' HCC/AOS
Odontoglossum pendulum
Oncidium Issaku Nagata 'Volcano Queen' HCC/AOS
Oncidium longipes
Oncidium Sharry Baby
Oncidium Sharry Baby 'Misaki'
Oncidium cheirophorum
Oncidium concolor
Oncidium cucullatum
Oncidium maculatum
Oncidium microchilum
Oncidium ornithorhynchum 'Lilac Blossom'
Paphiopedilum Armeni White
Paphiopedilum Joyce Hasagawa
Paphiopedilum Lynleigh Koopowitz
Paphiopedilum delenatii
Paphiopedilum emersonii
Paphiopedilum kolopakingii
Paphiopedilum malipoense
Phragmipedium Wilcox AM/AOS
Pleurothallis cocornaensis
Pleurothallis ramulosa
Polystachya Darling Star
Polystachya campyloglossa
Polystachya cultriformis
Polystachya fallax
Polystachya mazumbaiensis
Polystachya pubescens
Potinara Burana Beauty 'Burana'

HCC/AOS
Potinara Free Spirit 'Lea' AM/AOS
Potinara Twentyfour Carat 'Lea' AM/AOS
Rangaeris amaniensis
Rhyncholaelia digbyana
Sigmatostalix radicans 'HMO's Petite Prince'
Sophrolaeliocattleya Haw Yuan Star 'Pink Lady'
Stanhopea candida
Stanhopea cirrhata
Stanhopea costaricensis
Stanhopea ecornuta
Stanhopea embreei
Stanhopea grandiflora
Stanhopea jenischiana
Stanhopea oculata

Stanhopea pulla
Stanhopea reichenbachiana
Stanhopea saccata
Stanhopea tigrina
Stanhopea tricornis
Stanhopea wardii
Stelis pusilla
Trichocentrum albococcineum
Trichocentrum tigrinum
Trichoglottis philippinensis 'Pololei'
Trichopilia fragrans
Trichopilia suavis
Tuberolabium odoratissium
Vanda tricolor var. *suavis*
Woodwardara Adelaide
Zygoneria
Zygopetalum

Intermediate to Warm Temperature

Aerangis appendiculata
Aerangis articulata
Aerangis biloba
Aerangis brachycarpa
Aerangis citrata
Aerangis modesta
Aerangis mooreana
Aerangis mystacidii
Aeranthes Grandiose
Aerides crassifolia
Aerides falcata
Aerides falcata var. *houlletiana*
Aerides fieldingii
Aerides lawrenceae
Aerides lawrenceae var. *sanderiana*
Aerides odorata
Aerides quinquevulnera
Amesiella philippinense
Angraecum leonis
Ascofinetia Cherry Blossom 'Delicado'

Bothriochilus bellus
Brassavola cordata
Brassavola cucullata
Brassavola flagellaris
Brassavola Little Stars
Brassavola martiana
Brassavola nodosa
Brassavola tuberculata
Brassavola Yaki 'Black's Best'
Brassidium Dragon Flight 'Fluff'
Brassocattleya Binosa 'Kirk' AM/AOS
Brassocattleya Mt. Hood
Brassolaelia Sarah Black
Bulbophyllum comosum
Bulbophyllum echinolabium
Bulbophyllum hamatipes
Bulbophyllum laxiflorum
Bulbophyllum odoratissimum
Bulbophyllum rothschildianum
Cattleya forbesii

Cattleya guttata
Cattleya lueddemanniana 'Waterfield'
Cattleya luteola
Coelogyne cristata
Coryanthes bruckmuelleri
Coryanthes leucocorys
Cycnoches chlorochilon
Cycnoches loddigesii
Cycnoches ventricosum
Cycnoches warscewiczii
Dendrobium loddigesii
Dendrochilum magnum
Encyclia cordigera
Epidendrum difforme
Epilaelia Beverly Shea
Eria gigantea 'Waterfield'
Eurychone rothschildianum
Gongora galeata
Gongora grossa
Gongora horichiana
Gongora leucochila
Gongora pleiochroma
Gongora quinquenervis
Gongora unicolor
Laeliocattleya Whitiniae
Leptotes unicolor
Maxillaria ochroleuca
Maxillaria picta
Maxillaria rufescens

Neofinetia falcata
Neostylis Lou Sneary
Neostylis Lou Sneary 'Blue Moon'
Neostylis Lou Sneary 'Pinky'
    AM/AOS
Oncidium Gold Dust
Oncidium Tsiku Marguerite
Oncidium Twinkle 'Fragrance Fan-
    tasy'
Oncidium Twinkle 'Red Fantasy'
Oncidium crispum
Oncidium tigrinum
Otaara Haw Yuan Bay 'She Shu'
Peristeria elata
Phalaenopsis Orchid World 'Bonnie
    Vasquez' AM/AOS
Polystachya bella
Rhynchostylis gigantea
Rhynchostylis illustre
Ronnyara Manuel Ugarte 'H & R'
Spathoglottis deplanche
Trichocentrum Nathakhun
Trichoglottis wenzellii
Tuberolabium kotoense
Vanda Pat Delight
Vascostylis Crownfox Red Gem
Vascostylis Tham Yuen Hae 'Blue
    Queen' HCC/RSPC, JC/AOS,
    HCC/AOS

Warm Temperature (65°F/18°C and above)

Angraecum aporoides
Angraecum birrinense
Angraecum bosseri
Angraecum boisserianum
Angraecum compactum
Angraecum didieri
Angraecum distichum
Angraecum eburneum
Angraecum eichlerianum
Angraecum germinyanum

Angraecum Lemforde White Beauty
Angraecum Longiscott 'Lea'
Angraecum magdalenae
Angraecum sesquipedale
Angraecum Veitchii
Angraecum White Emblem
Ansellia africana
Arundina graminifolia
Brassia gireoudiana
Brassia longissima 'Pumpkin Patch'

Brassia verrucosa
Bulbophyllum lobbii
Coelogyne lawrenceana
Dendrobium anosmum
Dendrochilum cobbianum
Doritaenopsis Garnet Elf 'Mary'
Doritaenopsis Phoenix Fire 'Cardinal'
Oeniella polystachys
Phalaenopsis Caribbean Sunset 'Sweet Fragrance'
Phalaenopsis Desert Red 'Ruby'
Phalaenopsis Dotty Woodson 'Claudette' HCC/AOS
Phalaenopsis Ember 'Blumen Insel' AM/AOS
Phalaenopsis Kilby Cassviola 'Sweet Fragrance'
Phalaenopsis Mary Lillian Taylor 'Desert Orange' AM/AOS
Phalaenopsis Mini Mark
Phalaenopsis Orchid World 'Roman Holiday' AM/AOS
Phalaenopsis Perfection Is 'Chen' FCC/AOS
Phalaenopsis Samba
Phalaenopsis Sweet Memory 'Amy Dawn' AM/AOS
Phalaenopsis Valentinii

Phalaenopsis Wes Addison 'Blood Brother'
Phalaenopsis amboinensis
Phalaenopsis bellina
Phalaenopsis fasciata
Phalaenopsis gigantea
Phalaenopsis hieroglyphica
Phalaenopsis lueddemanniana
Phalaenopsis mannii
Phalaenopsis modesta
Phalaenopsis schilleriana
Phalaenopsis violacea
Rhyncholaelia glauca
Rhynchostylis coelestis
Rhynchostylis gigantea Sagarik Strain
Rhynchostylis gigantea var. *alba*
Rhynchostylis retusa
Schoenorchis fragrans
Schoenorchis gemmata
Sedirea japonica
Sobennikoffia humbertiana
Vanda coerulescens
Vanda dearei
Vanda denisoniana
Vanda roeblingiana
Vanda tesselata
Vanda tricolor

Orchids by Intensity of Fragrance

Although many orchids mentioned in this book have very strong, noticeable scents, some of them have light scents, which some growers may not be able to detect.

Light Fragrance

Acineta superba—light vanilla

Amesiella philippinense—minty

Angraecum distichum—jasmine

Ansellia africana—light floral

Arundina graminifolia—floral

Ascofinetia Cherry Blossom 'Delicado'—sweet floral

Beallara Marfitch 'Howard's Dream' AM/AOS—rose

Brassavola Yaki 'Black's Best'—musty-soapy; similar to the *B. cucullata* parent

Brassia gireoudiana—musky

Brassia longissima 'Pumpkin Patch'—light, sweet candy

Brassia verrucosa—musky

Brassidium Dragon Flight 'Fluff'—heliotrope

Brassocattleya Binosa 'Kirk' AM/AOS—spicy

Bulbophyllum ambrosia—honey, bitter almonds

Bulbophyllum comosum—hay scented

Bulbophyllum hamatipes—musky

Bulbophyllum laxiflorum—musky

Bulbophyllum rothschildianum—peach, fruity

Cadetia chionantha—sweet floral

Cadetia taylori—vanilla

Catasetum roseum—Vicks VapoRub in the morning, cinnamon at night

Cattleya Brabantiae—spicy

Cattleya Fascelis—spicy

Cattleya bicolor var. *grossii*—spicy, aromatic-floral, rose

Cattleya forbesii—fragrance of bubble gum

Cattleya granulosa—rosy-flora

Cattleya guttata—sweet floral

Cattleya harrisoniana—floral

Cattleya intermedia 'Carlos'—floral

Cattleya luteola—fresh floral

Cattleya mossiae—garlic

Cattleya schilleriana—honey
Cattleya warneri—clean, spicy
Cattleya warscewiczii—violets
Cirrhopetalum graveolens—carrion
Coelogyne lawrenceana—sweet floral
Coelogyne ochracea—musk
Coryanthes bruckmuelleri—herbal
Cymbidium Golden Elf 'Sundust' HCC/AOS—rose
Cymbidium cyperifolium—sweet
Cymbidium sinensis—light, sweet floral
Dendrobium Comet King 'Akatsuki'— sweet floral
Dendrobium Spring Bride—fresh, clean fragrance
Dendrobium Spring Doll—fresh, clean fragrance
Dendrobium Sweet Song 'Memory'— fresh, clean fragrance
Dendrobium bellatulum—lemon, orange
Dendrobium chrysotoxum—pineapple, melon, mango
Dendrobium jenkinsii—honey
Dendrobium lawesii—floral
Dendrobium loddigesii—sweet floral
Dendrobium macrophyllum—sweet floral
Dendrobium nobile—honey, musk by day; mown hay at night
Dendrobium nobile var. virginale— floral
Dendrobium parishii—rhubarb, raspberry
Doritaenopsis Garnet Elf 'Mary'— sweet floral
Doritaenopsis Phoenix Fire 'Cardinal'—sweet floral
Dracula chestertonii—fungus
Encyclia adenocaula—floral
Encyclia polybulbon—sandalwood, cloves

Epidendrum difforme—medicinal
Epidendrum parkinsonianum—spicy to floral
Epilaelia Beverly Shea—sweet floral
Gongora horichiana—sweet floral
Gongora leucochila—spicy, nutmeg
Gongora pleiochroma—powdered cocoa, lilac, hyacinth, sweet floral
Gongora quinquenervis—cinnamon, cloves, lily of the valley
Gongora unicolor—chocolate flavored corn chips, sweet, cocoa
Iwanagaara Appleblossom 'Fantastic'—sweet floral
Jumellea confusa—jasmine
Jumellea densifoliata—jasmine
Laelia albida—primrose
Laelia anceps—primrose, vanilla
Laelia lundii—floral scent
Laelia perrinii—spicy floral
Laelia pumila var. coerulea—light floral
Laelia tenebrosa—spicy
Laeliocattleya Mini Purple—Charles Marden Fitch describes it as "light spicy blend with undertones of dusky cloves"
Laeliocattleya Whitiniae—sweet floral
Leptotes bicolor—vanilla
Leptotes unicolor—sweet floral
Lycaste Alan Salzman—spicy
Lycaste Aquila 'Détente' FCC/AOS— sweet floral
Lycaste Imschootiana—spicy
Lycaste bradeorum—lemon
Lycaste brevispatha—fresh apples
Lycaste ciliata—ripe apples
Lycaste cochleata—oranges
Masdevallia Confetti—spicy, "like Necco wafers"
Masdevallia agaster—floral

Masdevallia attenuata—floral
Masdevallia cyclotega—floral
Masdevallia laucheana—rosy-floral
Masdevallia livingstoneana—fruity
scent
Masdevallia mejiana—spice
Maxillaria ochroleuca—tutti-frutti
Maxillaria picta—sweet floral
Maxillaria rufescens—vanilla, egg
crème
Maxillaria sanderiana—sweet floral
Meiracyllium trinasutum—cinnamon
Milpasia Leslie Garay—rosy-flora
Miltoniopsis Bert Field—light floral
Miltoniopsis Celle 'Wasserfall'
AM/AOS—rosy-flora
Miltoniopsis Hajime Ono—light rose
Miltoniopsis Hamburg 'Red Velvet'—
rosy-flora
Miltoniopsis santanaei—rosy
Neostylis Lou Sneary—vanilla candy
Neostylis Lou Sneary 'Pinky'
AM/AOS—vanilla, candy
Odontioda Vesta 'Charm'—citrus
Odontobrassia Fangtastic Bob
Henley—floral
Odontocidium Tiger Crow 'Golden
Girl' HCC/AOS—light floral
Oncidium Gold Dust—floral
Oncidium Issaku Nagata 'Volcano
Queen' HCC/AOS—light floral
Oncidium Tsiku Marguerite—sweet,
soapy
Oncidium concolor—spiced apple pie
Oncidium crispum—musty, "like
cockroaches"
Oncidium microchilum—cider
Otaara Haw Yuan Bay 'She Shu'—
vanilla
Paphiopedilum Armeni White—
citrus
Paphiopedilum Joyce Hasagawa—
raspberry

Paphiopedilum Lynleigh Koopowitz—
raspberry
Paphiopedilum delenatii—roses,
lemon honey
Paphiopedilum emersonii—chocolate
Paphiopedilum kolopakingii—honey-
suckle
Paphiopedilum malipoense—rasp-
berry, apple
Peristeria elata—citrus, eucalyptus
Phalaenopsis Caribbean Sunset
'Sweet Fragrance'—rose floral
Phalaenopsis Desert Red 'Ruby'—
sweet
Phalaenopsis Dotty Woodson
'Claudette' HCC/AOS—sweet
Phalaenopsis Ember 'Blumen Insel'
AM/AOS—rose floral
Phalaenopsis Kilby Cassviola 'Sweet
Fragrance'—spicy
Phalaenopsis Mary Lillian Taylor
'Desert Orange' AM/AOS—spicy
Phalaenopsis Mini Mark 'Holm'—
sweet floral
Phalaenopsis Samba—sweet floral
Phalaenopsis Valentinii—freesia
Phalaenopsis Wes Addison 'Blood
Brother'—floral
Phalaenopsis amboinensis—musk
Phalaenopsis fasciata—rosy-floral
Phalaenopsis gigantea—orange peel
Phalaenopsis hieroglyphica—rosy-
floral
Phalaenopsis lueddemanniana—sweet
Phalaenopsis mannii—mandarin
orange
Phalaenopsis schilleriana—rose petals
Phalaenopsis violacea—floral with a
touch of spice and cinnamon
Phragmipedium Wilcox AM/AOS—
roses
Pleurothallis cocornaensis—moldy
socks

Pleurothallis ramulosa—sweet
Polystachya Darling Star—floral
Polystachya bella—fruity, "like Lemon Pledge"
Potinara Free Spirit 'Lea' AM/AOS—sweet floral
Schoenorchis fragrans—sweet
Schoenorchis gemmata—sweet
Sedirea japonica—clean and fresh lemon fragrance
Sigmatostalix radicans 'HMO's Petite Prince'—honey
Spathoglottis deplanche—fragrance of grape soda
Stanhopea candida—sweet
Stanhopea cirrhata—Vicks

Stanhopea pulla—lemon-lime candy, cool minty, citrus
Stelis pusilla—sweet
Thunia marshalliana—orange
Trichocentrum albococcineum—floral
Trichoglottis philippinensis 'Pololei'—ripe apples
Trichoglottis wenzellii—sweet
Vanda Pat Delight—ripe grapes
Vanda cristata—floral
Vanda roeblingiana—sweet
Vascostylis Tham Yuen Hae 'Blue Queen' HCC/RSPC, JC/AOS, HCC/AOS—jasmine
Zygopetalum maxillare—floral

Strong Fragrance

Acampe papillosa—hyacinths
Aerangis appendiculata—gardenia
Aerangis articulata—jasmine
Aerangis biloba—gardenia, lily
Aerangis brachycarpa—vanilla, jasmine
Aerangis citrata—lemon
Aerangis confusa—tuberose, gardenia
Aerangis fastuosa—tuberose, lily
Aerangis kirkii—tuberose, gardenia
Aerangis kotschyana—gardenia
Aerangis modesta—minty spice
Aerangis mooreana—jasmine
Aerangis mystacidii—lily of the valley
Aerangis somalensis—gardenia
Aeranthes Grandiose—jasmine
Aerides crassifolia—aromatic floral
Aerides falcata—citrus, fruity
Aerides falcata var. *houlletiana*—citrus, fruity
Aerides fieldingii—lily-of-the-valley, cyclamen
Aerides lawrenceae—lemon-spice, honey, anise

Aerides lawrenceae var. *sanderiana*—lemon-spice
Aerides odorata—spicy; ribbon candy, cloves, lilac
Aerides quinquevulnera—cinnamon
Angraecum aporoides—gardenia
Angraecum birrinense—orange blossom
Angraecum bosseri—spicy floral
Angraecum compactum—spicy, citrusy
Angraecum didieri—sweet, spicy
Angraecum germinyanum—jasmine
Angraecum leonis—jasmine
Angraecum magdalenae—jasmine
Angraecum sesquipedale—jasmine
Angraecum Veitchii—jasmine
Angraecum White Emblem—jasmine
Angranthes Grandalena—jasmine
Anguloa clowesii—chocolate and mint, paste, coconut, citrus
Bifrenaria harrisoniae—fruity

Bothriochilus bellus—almond/poppy pastry filling

Brassavola Little Stars—soapy-sweet

Brassavola cordata—soapy-sweet

Brassavola cucullata—musty-soapy

Brassavola martiana—soapy-sweet

Brassavola nodosa—freesia, lily-of-the-valley

Brassavola tuberculata—nicotiana, gardenia

Brassia ochroleuca—spicy, spiced apple pie

Brassocattleya Mt. Hood—vanilla

Brassolaelia Memoria Bernice Foster—sweet floral

Brassolaelia Yellow Bird—citrus to spicy

Brassolaeliocattleya Arthur Bossin 'Rapture'—sweet floral

Brassolaeliocattleya Formosan Gold—vanilla

Brassolaeliocattleya George King 'Serendipity' AM/AOS—vanilla

Brassolaeliocattleya Goldenzelle 'Lemon Chiffon' AM/AOS—sweet floral

Brassolaeliocattleya Haw Yuan Beauty 'Orchis'—vanilla

Brassolaeliocattleya Hawaiian Avalanche—sweet floral, vanilla

Brassolaeliocattleya Momilani Rainbow—sweet floral

Brassolaeliocattleya Pamela Hetherington 'Coronation' FCC/AOS—sweet floral

Brassolaeliocattleya Ports of Paradise 'Emerald Isle' HCC/AOS—citrus

Brassolaeliocattleya Rio's Green Magic—citrus

Bulbophyllum cocoinum—coconut

Bulbophyllum echinolabium—carrion

Bulbophyllum lobbii—jasmine, orange blossoms

Bulbophyllum maximum—musky

Bulbophyllum odoratissimum—pleasant fragrance

Bulbophyllum phalaenopsis—carrion

Bulbophyllum suavissimum—musky

Catasetum Orchidglade 'Davie Ranches' AM/AOS—spicy, medicinal

Catasetum candida—wintergreen

Catasetum collare—wintergreen

Catasetum discolor—rye bread

Catasetum expansum—turpentine in morning; rye bread in afternoon

Catasetum gnomus—wintergreen

Catasetum integerrimum—spice

Catasetum maculatum—rye bread

Catasetum tenebrosum—citrus

Catasetum warscewiczii—lemon

Cattleya Chocolate Drop 'Kodama' AM/AOS—lily-of-the-valley, citrus, roses, lilies

Cattleya Peckhaviensis—honey

Cattleya Pradit Spot 'Black Prince'—sweet floral

Cattleya aclandiae—spicy

Cattleya dowiana—lemon, soapy, spicy, vanilla

Cattleya intermedia—sweet floral

Cattleya labiata—spicy, aromatic, cloves

Cattleya loddigesii—baked milk chocolate

Cattleya lueddemanniana 'Waterfield'—floral

Cattleya maxima 'Mountainside'—heliotrope, sweet pea

Cattleya quadicolor—ripe plums

Cattleya schroederae—almonds

Cattleya walkeriana var. *alba*—vanilla, cinnamon

Caularthron bicornutum—fruit, candy, cotton candy, raspberries, strawberries

Cirrhopetalum ornatissimum—said by Linet Hamman to smell like whale oil, while the lip smells like fresh herring

Cochleanthes Moliere—candy, rose

Cochleanthes discolor—candy, cedar, pepper, camphoraceous

Coelogyne Intermedia—sweet, fruity

Coelogyne cristata Banana, candy sweet

Coelogyne fimbriata—yeasty

Coelogyne pandurata—cinnamon

Coelogyne zurowetzii—spicy floral

Cycnoches—vanilla, spice

Cycnoches chlorochilon—jasmine

Cycnoches loddigesii—jasmine

Cycnoches ventricosum—jasmine

Cycnoches warscewiczii—ripe fruit

Cymbidium eburneum—sweet, like paperwhite narcissus

Cymbidium ensifolium—citrus, lemony scent with a touch of jasmine

Cymbidium goeringii—jasmine, lily-of-the valley, lemons

Cymbidium kanran—lemon peel

Cymbidium mastersii—almonds

Cymbidium suave—sweet

Cymbidium tracyanum—peach

Cymbidium virescens—the sweet, delicate fragrance earned it the moniker of "the scent of the king"

Darwinara Charm 'Blue Star'—vanilla

Dendrobium Chrystaline—hyacinths

Dendrobium Gai Quest—sweet floral

Dendrobium Jesmond Fancy—sweet floral

Dendrobium Jesmond Gem—sweet floral

Dendrobium Light River—sweet floral

Dendrobium Sea Mary 'Snow King'—sweet floral

Dendrobium anosmum raspberry

Dendrobium antennatum—rosy-flora

Dendrobium aureum—fruity, violets

Dendrobium cariniferum—tangerines

Dendrobium delicatum 'Brechts'—wintergreen

Dendrobium densiflorum—honey

Dendrobium draconis—mandarins, tangerines

Dendrobium fimbriatum var. *oculatum*—sweet

Dendrobium griffithianum—spicy-floral

Dendrobium hainanense—honey

Dendrobium heterocarpum—honeysuckle, primrose

Dendrobium kingianum—floral, hyacinth, lilac, honey

Dendrobium moniliforme—rosy-floral

Dendrobium monophyllum—rosy-floral, jasmine, fruity

Dendrobium musciferum—vanilla

Dendrobium primulinum var. *giganteum*—primrose

Dendrobium pugioniforme—vanilla

Dendrobium rhodopterygium var. *semialba*—sweet floral

Dendrobium speciosum—hyacinth

Dendrobium unicum—peach, apricot

Dendrobium virgineum—gardenia, rose, woody

Dendrobium wardianum—caramel

Dendrobium williamsonii—spicy, citrus

Dendrochilum cobbianum—fresh, vanilla

Dendrochilum arachnites—cinnamon

Dendrochilum magnum—sweet "wheaty" or spicy scent

Diaphananthe pellucida—heavy floral sweet scent

Diaphananthe pulchella—gardenia

Encyclia citrina—lemon
Encyclia cordigera—honey and vanilla
Encyclia fragrans—honey, vanilla, gardenias, magnolias, lilac
Encyclia lancifolia—spicy
Encyclia phoenicea—chocolate
Encyclia radiata—spicy floral, coconut cream pie, lilac, carnation, hyacinth
Encyclia tampensis—honey
Encyclia trulla—spice
Epicattleya Dora Tinschert 'Springdale' HCC/AOS—sweet floral
Epidendrum ciliare—white floral, grapefruit
Epidendrum falcatum—jasmine, Easter lily
Epidendrum inversum—cloves
Epidendrum nocturnum—eucalyptus, aniseed
Epidendrum phoeniceum—chocolate
Eria gigantea 'Waterfield'—citrus
Eria hyacinthoides—carrion
Eurychone rothschildianum—cinnamon
Gongora galeata—orange
Gongora grossa—fishy, stale, musty, sweaty gym clothes
Haraella odorata—citrus
Jumellea sagittata—floral, jasmine
Laelia purpurata var. *werckhauseri*—spice, anise
Laelia rubescens—wintergreen
Laeliocattleya Angel Love—citrusy
Laeliocattleya Hausermann's Sultan—cloves
Laeliocattleya Jungle Festival—sweet floral
Laeliocattleya Mari's Song 'CTM 217' HCC/AOS—sweet floral
Laeliocattleya Nora's Melody—sweet floral

Lycaste Lucianii—sweet and spicy
Lycaste Walnut Valley 'Black's Glow'—spicy
Lycaste deppei—peppermint, eucalyptus
Lycaste locusta—Granny Smith apples
Masdevallia glandulosa—cloves
Masdevallia triangularis—musty, repugnant
Maxillaria seymouriana—lemony
Maxillaria tenuifolia—coconut; box of crayons
Milpasia Milt's Choice 'Helen of Troy'—rosy-floral
Miltonia regnellii—oranges, coriander
Miltonia schroederiana—spice floral, carnation
Miltonia spectabilis—rose, spicy
Miltonia spectabilis var. *moreliana*—rose, spicy
Miltoniopsis phalaenopsis—rose, lily-of-the-valley, cyclamen
Miltoniopsis roezlii—fruity, rose
Neofinetia falcata—jasmine, vanilla
Neostylis Lou Sneary 'Blue Moon'—jasmine
Odontoglossum pendulum—lemony rose
Odontoglossum pulchellum—vanilla, rosy-floral
Oeniella polystachys—vanilla; lily-of-the-valley
Oncidium cucullatum—violet
Oncidium longipes—aniseed, cinnamon, floral
Oncidium maculatum—honey
Oncidium ornithorhynchum 'Lilac Blossom'—vanilla, "like a fresh morning," baby powder, grape, spicy, cinnamon, cocoa, candy-sweet

Oncidium Sharry Baby 'Misaki'—chocolate, vanilla

Oncidium tigrinum—vanilla, freesia

Oncidium Twinkle 'Fragrance Fantasy'—sweet

Oncidium Twinkle 'Red Fantasy'—sweet

Phalaenopsis Orchid World 'Bonnie Vasquez' AM/AOS—spicy

Phalaenopsis Orchid World 'Roman Holiday' AM/AOS—spicy

Phalaenopsis Perfection Is 'Chen' FCC/AOS—spicy, cloves, carnation

Phalaenopsis Sweet Memory 'Amy Dawn' AM/AOS—freesia

Phalaenopsis bellina—freesia, lily of the valley, rose cologne, touch of velvet, lemon

Phalaenopsis modesta—honeysuckle, lilac, grapes, sweet candy

Polystachya campyloglossa—bananas, strawberries

Polystachya cultriformis—lily-of-the-valley, lime blossoms

Polystachya fallax—jasmine, tropical fruit

Polystachya mazumbaiensis—rose, gardenia

Polystachya pubescens—honey

Potinara Burana Beauty 'Burana' HCC/AOS—citrus

Potinara Twentyfour Carat 'Lea' AM/AOS—vanilla

Rangaeris amaniensis—lily-of-the-valley, lily

Rhyncholaelia digbyana—lily-of-the-valley, lemon

Rhyncholaelia glauca—rose, lily-of-the-valley, cyclamen

Rhynchostylis coelestis—citrus

Rhynchostylis gigantea—citrus

Rhynchostylis gigantea Sagarik Strain—citrus

Rhynchostylis gigantea var. *alba*—citrus

Rhynchostylis illustre—citrus

Rhynchostylis retusa—citrus

Ronnyara Manuel Ugarte 'H & R'—sweet floral

Sobennikoffia humbertiana—spice

Sophrolaeliocattleya Haw Yuan Star 'Pink Lady'—sweet, floral

Stanhopea ecornuta—fresh floral, cinnamon

Stanhopea embreei—chocolate

Stanhopea oculata—chocolate

Stanhopea reichenbachiana—jasmine

Stanhopea saccata—cinnamon

Stanhopea tricornis—jasmine

Trichocentrum Nathakhun—honey

Trichocentrum tigrinum—lily-of-the-valley

Trichopilia fragrans—narcissus

Trichopilia suavis—floral; intoxicating

Tuberolabium kotoense—floral

Vanda coerulescens—like grape bubblegum, concord grapes

Vanda dearei—vanilla, cinnamon

Vanda denisoniana—sweet

Vanda tesselata—grapes, lilac

Vanda tricolor—vanilla

Vanda tricolor var. *suavis*—vanilla

Vascostylis Crownfox Red Gem—citrusy

Woodwardara Adelaide—sweet

Zygocolax—sweet

Zygoneria—hyacinth

Zygopetalum—sweet

Zygopetalum Artur Elle 'Tanzanite' AM/AOS—hyacinths, violets, sweet perfume

Zygopetalum BG White 'Stonehurst' HCC/AOS, AM/AOS—hyacinths, violets, sweet perfume

Zygopetalum Redvale 'Fire Kiss'—hyacinth

Zygopetalum crinitum—spicy-floral, narcissus

Zygopetalum intermedium—rose, lilac

Zygopetalum mackayi—hyacinth, narcissus

Very Strong Fragrance

Angraecum Lemforde White Beauty—jasmine

Angraecum Longiscott 'Lea'—jasmine

Angraecum boisserianum—jasmine

Angraecum eburneum—gardenia

Angraecum eichlerianum—jasmine, lily

Brassavola flagellaris—hot chocolate

Brassolaelia Sarah Black—very sweet floral

Bulbophyllum beccarii—said to smell like 100 dead elephants rotting in the sun

Catasetum fimbriatum—spice

Cochleanthes amazonica—candy, rose, narcissus, verbena

Coryanthes leucocorys—mint

Dendrochilum glumaceum—curry

Lycaste aromatica—cinnamon, spicy, like Big Red chewing gum

Lycaste cruenta—spicy, cinnamon, lemon, cloves

Lycaste lanipes—heady, honey perfume

Lycaste leucantha—sweet, heady perfume

Lycaste powellii—sweet floral

Oncidium cheirophorum—citrus, lemon

Stanhopea costaricensis—very sweet, cloves, baby powder, spicy

Stanhopea grandiflora—jasmine

Stanhopea jenischiana—cinnamon, fruity

Stanhopea tigrina—sweet

Stanhopea wardii—jasmine, floral hand soap, candy, chocolate

Tuberolabium odoratissium—sweet

Orchids by Time of Fragrance

Day

Acampe papillosa
Acineta superba
Aerangis fastuosa
Aerides crassifolia
Aerides falcata
Aerides falcata var. houlletiana
Aerides fieldingii
Aerides lawrenceae
Aerides lawrenceae var. sanderiana
Aerides odorata
Aerides quinquevulnera
Anguloa clowesii
Ansellia africana
Arundina graminifolia
Ascofinetia Cherry Blossom 'Delicado'
Beallara Marfitch 'Howard's Dream'
   AM/AOS
Bifrenaria harrisoniae
Bothriochilus bellus
Brassia gireoudiana
Brassia longissima 'Pumpkin Patch'
Brassia ochroleuca
Brassia verrucosa
Brassidium Dragon Flight 'Fluff'
Brassocattleya Mt. Hood
Brassolaeliocattleya Arthur Bossin
   'Rapture'
Brassolaeliocattleya Formosan
   Gold
Brassolaeliocattleya George King
   'Serendipity' AM/AOS
Brassolaeliocattleya Goldenzelle
   'Lemon Chiffon' AM/AOS
Brassolaeliocattleya Haw Yuan
   Beauty 'Orchis'
Brassolaeliocattleya Hawaiian
   Avalanche
Brassolaeliocattleya Momilani
   Rainbow
Brassolaeliocattleya Pamela Hether-
   ington 'Coronation' FCC/AOS
Brassolaeliocattleya Ports of Paradise
   'Emerald Isle' HCC/AOS
Bulbophyllum ambrosia
Bulbophyllum beccarii
Bulbophyllum cocoinum
Bulbophyllum comosum
Bulbophyllum echinolabium
Bulbophyllum hamatipes
Bulbophyllum laxiflorum
Bulbophyllum lobbii
Bulbophyllum maximum
Bulbophyllum odoratissimum
Bulbophyllum phalaenopsis

Bulbophyllum rothschildianum
Bulbophyllum suavissimum
Cadetia chionantha
Cadetia taylori
Catasetum Orchidglade 'Davie
    Ranches' AM/AOS
Catasetum candida
Catasetum collare
Catasetum discolor
Catasetum expansum
Catasetum fimbriatum
Catasetum gnomus
Catasetum integerrimum
Catasetum maculatum
Catasetum roseum
Catasetum tenebrosum
Catasetum warscewiczii
Cattleya Brabantiae
Cattleya Chocolate Drop 'Kodama'
    AM/AOS
Cattleya Fascelis
Cattleya Peckhaviensis
Cattleya Pradit Spot 'Black Prince'
Cattleya aclandiae
Cattleya bicolor var. grossii
Cattleya dowiana
Cattleya forbesii
Cattleya granulosa
Cattleya guttata
Cattleya harrisoniana
Cattleya intermedia
Cattleya intermedia 'Carlos'
Cattleya labiata
Cattleya loddigesii
Cattleya lueddemanniana 'Waterfield'
Cattleya luteola
Cattleya maxima 'Mountainside'
Cattleya mossiae
Cattleya quadicolor
Cattleya schilleriana
Cattleya schroederae
Cattleya walkeriana var. alba

Cattleya warneri
Cattleya warscewiczii
Caularthron bicornutum
Cirrhopetalum graveolens
Cirrhopetalum ornatissimum
Cochleanthes Moliere
Cochleanthes amazonica
Cochleanthes discolor
Coelogyne Intermedia
Coelogyne cristata
Coelogyne fimbriata
Coelogyne lawrenceana
Coelogyne ochracea
Coelogyne pandurata
Coelogyne zurowetzii
Coryanthes bruckmuelleri
Coryanthes leucocorys
Cycnoches
Cycnoches chlorochilon
Cycnoches loddigesii
Cycnoches ventricosum
Cycnoches warscewiczii
Cymbidium Golden Elf 'Sundust'
    HCC/AOS
Cymbidium cyperifolium
Cymbidium eburneum
Cymbidium ensifolium
Cymbidium goeringii
Cymbidium kanran
Cymbidium mastersii
Cymbidium sinensis
Cymbidium suave
Cymbidium tracyanum
Cymbidium virescens
Darwinara Charm 'Blue Star'
Dendrobium Chrystaline
Dendrobium Comet King 'Akatsuki'
Dendrobium Gai Quest
Dendrobium Jesmond Fancy
Dendrobium Jesmond Gem
Dendrobium Light River
Dendrobium Sea Mary 'Snow King'

Dendrobium Spring Bride
Dendrobium Spring Doll
Dendrobium—Sweet Song 'Memory'
Dendrobium anosmum
Dendrobium antennatum
Dendrobium aureum
Dendrobium bellatulum
Dendrobium cariniferum
Dendrobium chrysotoxum
Dendrobium delicatum 'Brechts'
Dendrobium densiflorum
Dendrobium draconis
Dendrobium fimbriatum var.
   oculatum
Dendrobium griffithianum
Dendrobium hainanense
Dendrobium heterocarpum
Dendrobium jenkinsii
Dendrobium kingianum
Dendrobium lawesii
Dendrobium loddigesii
Dendrobium macrophyllum
Dendrobium moniliforme
Dendrobium monophyllum
Dendrobium musciferum
Dendrobium nobile
Dendrobium nobile var. virginale
Dendrobium parishii
Dendrobium primulinum var.
   giganteum
Dendrobium pugioniforme
Dendrobium rhodopterygium var.
   semialba
Dendrobium speciosum
Dendrobium unicum
Dendrobium virgineum
Dendrobium wardianum
Dendrobium williamsonii
Dendrochilum cobbianum
Dendrochilum glumaceum
Dendrochilum arachnites
Dendrochilum magnum

Doritaenopsis Garnet Elf 'Mary'
Doritaenopsis Phoenix Fire 'Cardinal'
Dracula chestertonii
Encyclia adenocaula
Encyclia citrina
Encyclia cordigera
Encyclia fragrans
Encyclia lancifolia
Encyclia phoenicea
Encyclia polybulbon
Encyclia radiata
Encyclia tampensis
Encyclia trulla
Epicattleya Dora Tinschert 'Spring-
   dale' HCC/AOS
Epidendrum difforme
Epidendrum falcatum
Epidendrum inversum
Epidendrum parkinsonianum
Epidendrum phoeniceum
Epilaelia Beverly Shea
Eria gigantea 'Waterfield'
Eria hyacinthoides
Eurychone rothschildianum
Gongora galeata
Gongora grossa
Gongora horichiana
Gongora leucochila
Gongora pleiochroma
Gongora quinquenervis
Gongora unicolor
Haraella odorata
Iwanagaara Appleblossom 'Fantastic'
Laelia albida
Laelia anceps
Laelia lundii
Laelia perrinii
Laelia pumila var. coerulea
Laelia purpurata var. werckhauseri
Laelia rubescens
Laelia tenebrosa
Laeliocattleya Angel Love

Laeliocattleya Angel Love
Laeliocattleya Hausermann's Sultan
Laeliocattleya Jungle Festival
Laeliocattleya Mari's Song 'CTM 217' HCC/AOS
Laeliocattleya Mini Purple
Laeliocattleya Nora's Melody
Laeliocattleya Whitiniae
Leptotes bicolor
Leptotes unicolor
Lycaste Alan Salzman
Lycaste Aquila 'Détente' FCC/AOS
Lycaste Imschootiana
Lycaste Lucianii
Lycaste Walnut Valley 'Black's Glow'
Lycaste aromatica
Lycaste bradeorum
Lycaste brevispatha
Lycaste ciliata
Lycaste cochleata
Lycaste cruenta
Lycaste deppei
Lycaste lanipes
Lycaste leucantha
Lycaste locusta
Lycaste powellii
Masdevallia Confetti
Masdevallia agaster
Masdevallia attenuata
Masdevallia cyclotega
Masdevallia glandulosa
Masdevallia livingstoneana
Masdevallia mejiana
Masdevallia triangularis
Maxillaria ochroleuca
Maxillaria picta
Maxillaria rufescens
Maxillaria sanderiana
Maxillaria seymouriana
Maxillaria tenuifolia
Meiracyllium trinasutum
Milpasia Leslie Garay

Milpasia Milt's Choice 'Helen of Troy'
Miltonia regnellii
Miltonia schroederiana
Miltonia spectabilis
Miltonia spectabilis var. *moreliana*
Miltoniopsis Bert Field
Miltoniopsis Celle 'Wasserfall' AM/AOS
Miltoniopsis Hajime Ono
Miltoniopsis Hamburg 'Red Velvet'
Miltoniopsis phalaenopsis
Miltoniopsis roezlii
Miltoniopsis santanaei
Neofinetia falcata
Neostylis Lou Sneary
Neostylis Lou Sneary 'Blue Moon'
Neostylis Lou Sneary 'Pinky' AM/AOS
Odontioda Vesta 'Charm'
Odontobrassia Fangtastic Bob Henley
Odontocidium Tiger Crow 'Golden Girl' HCC/AOS
Odontoglossum pendulum
Odontoglossum pulchellum
Oeniella polystachys
Oncidium Issaku Nagata 'Volcano Queen' HCC/AOS
Oncidium longipes
Oncidium Gold Dust
Oncidium Sharry Baby
Oncidium Sharry Baby 'Misaki'
Oncidium Tsiku Marguerite
Oncidium Twinkle 'Fragrance Fantasy'
Oncidium Twinkle 'Red Fantasy'
Oncidium cheirophorum
Oncidium concolor
Oncidium crispum
Oncidium cucullatum
Oncidium maculatum

Oncidium microchilum
Oncidium ornithorhynchum 'Lilac
   Blossom'
Otaara Haw Yuan Bay 'She Shu'
Paphiopedilum Armeni White
Paphiopedilum Joyce Hasagawa
Paphiopedilum Lynleigh Koopowitz
Paphiopedilum delenatii
Paphiopedilum emersonii
Paphiopedilum kolopakingii
Paphiopedilum malipoense
Peristeria elata
Phalaenopsis Caribbean Sunset
   'Sweet Fragrance'
Phalaenopsis Desert Red 'Ruby'
Phalaenopsis Dotty Woodson
   'Claudette' HCC/AOS
Phalaenopsis Ember 'Blumen Insel'
   AM/AOS
Phalaenopsis Kilby Cassviola 'Sweet
   Fragrance'
Phalaenopsis Mary Lillian Taylor
   'Desert Orange' AM/AOS
Phalaenopsis Mini Mark 'Holm'
Phalaenopsis Orchid World 'Bonnie
   Vasquez' AM/AOS
Phalaenopsis Orchid World 'Roman
   Holiday' AM/AOS
Phalaenopsis Perfection Is 'Chen'
   FCC/AOS
Phalaenopsis Samba
Phalaenopsis Sweet Memory 'Amy
   Dawn' AM/AOS
Phalaenopsis Valentinii
Phalaenopsis Wes Addison 'Blood
   Brother'
Phalaenopsis amboinensis
Phalaenopsis bellina
Phalaenopsis fasciata
Phalaenopsis gigantea
Phalaenopsis hieroglyphica
Phalaenopsis lueddemanniana

Phalaenopsis mannii
Phalaenopsis modesta
Phalaenopsis schilleriana
Phalaenopsis violacea
Phragmipedium Wilcox AM/AOS
Pleurothallis cocornaensis
Pleurothallis ramulosa
Polystachya Darling Star
Polystachya bella
Polystachya pubescens
Potinara Burana Beauty 'Burana'
   HCC/AOS
Potinara Free Spirit 'Lea' AM/AOS
Potinara Twentyfour Carat 'Lea'
   AM/AOS
Rhynchostylis coelestis
Rhynchostylis gigantea
Rhynchostylis gigantea Sagarik Strain
Rhynchostylis gigantea var. alba
Rhynchostylis illustre
Rhynchostylis retusa
Ronnyara Manuel Ugarte 'H & R'
Schoenorchis fragrans
Schoenorchis gemmata
Sedirea japonica
Sigmatostalix radicans 'HMO's Petite
   Prince'
Sobennikoffia humbertiana
Sophrolaeliocattleya Haw Yuan Star
   'Pink Lady'
Spathoglottis deplanche
Stanhopea candida
Stanhopea cirrhata
Stanhopea costaricensis
Stanhopea ecornuta
Stanhopea embreei
Stanhopea grandiflora
Stanhopea jenischiana
Stanhopea oculata
Stanhopea pulla
Stanhopea reichenbachiana
Stanhopea saccata

Stanhopea tigrina
Stanhopea tricornis
Stanhopea wardii
Stelis pusilla
Thunia marshalliana
Trichocentrum albococcineum
Trichocentrum Nathakhun
Trichocentrum tigrinum
Trichoglottis philippinensis 'Pololei'
Trichoglottis wenzellii
Trichopilia suavis
Tuberolabium kotoense
Tuberolabium odoratissium
Vanda Pat Delight
Vanda coerulescens
Vanda cristata
Vanda dearei
Vanda roeblingiana
Vanda tesselata

Vanda tricolor
Vanda tricolor var. suavis
Vascostylis Crownfox Red Gem
Vascostylis Tham Yuen Hae 'Blue
    Queen' HCC/RSPC, JC/AOS,
    HCC/AOS
Woodwardara Adelaide
Zygocolax
Zygoneria
Zygopetalum
Zygopetalum Artur Elle 'Tanzanite'
    AM/AOS
Zygopetalum BG White 'Stonehurst'
    HCC/AOS, AM/AOS
Zygopetalum Redvale 'Fire Kiss'
Zygopetalum crinitum
Zygopetalum intermedium
Zygopetalum mackayi
Zygopetalum maxillare

Evening

Aerangis appendiculata
Aerangis articulata
Aerangis biloba
Aerangis brachycarpa
Aerangis citrata
Aerangis confusa
Aerangis kirkii
Aerangis kotschyana
Aerangis modesta
Aerangis mooreana
Aerangis mystacidii
Aerangis somalensis
Aeranthes Grandiose
Amesiella philippinense
Angraecum aporoides
Angraecum birrinense
Angraecum bosseri
Angraecum boisserianum
Angraecum compactum
Angraecum didieri

Angraecum distichum
Angraecum eburneum
Angraecum eichlerianum
Angraecum germinyanum
Angraecum Lemforde White Beauty
Angraecum leonis
Angraecum Longiscott 'Lea'
Angraecum magdalenae
Angraecum sesquipedale
Angraecum Veitchii
Angraecum White Emblem
Angranthes Grandalena
Brassavola Little Stars
Brassavola Yaki 'Black's Best'
Brassavola cordata
Brassavola cucullata
Brassavola flagellaris
Brassavola martiana
Brassavola nodosa
Brassavola tuberculata

Brassocattleya Binosa 'Kirk' AM/AOS
Brassolaelia Memoria Bernice Foster
Brassolaelia Sarah Black
Brassolaelia Yellow Bird
Brassolaeliocattleya Rio's Green Magic
Diaphananthe pellucida
Diaphananthe pulchella
Epidendrum ciliare
Epidendrum nocturnum
Jumellea confusa
Jumellea densifoliata
Jumellea sagittata

Masdevallia laucheana
Oncidium tigrinum
Polystachya campyloglossa
Polystachya cultriformis
Polystachya fallax
Polystachya mazumbaiensis
Rangaeris amaniensis
Rhyncholaelia digbyana
Rhyncholaelia glauca
Trichopilia fragrans
Vanda denisoniana

Appendix F

Orchids by Season of Bloom

Spring Blooming

Aerangis citrata
Aerangis fastuosa
Aerangis modesta
Angraecum germinyanum
Angraecum White Emblem
Arundina graminifolia
Bifrenaria harrisoniae
Brassia gireoudiana
Brassia ochroleuca
Bulbophyllum maximum
Catasetum tenebrosum
Cattleya Pradit Spot 'Black Prince'
Cattleya bicolor var. *grossii*
Cattleya loddigesii
Cattleya lueddemanniana 'Waterfield'
Cattleya luteola
Cattleya schroederae
Caularthron bicornutum
Coelogyne ochracea
Cymbidium goeringii
Cymbidium suave
Cymbidium virescens
Dendrobium cariniferum
Dendrobium densiflorum
Dendrobium fimbriatum var. *oculatum*
Dendrobium griffithianum

Dendrobium hainanense
Dendrobium kingianum
Dendrobium loddigesii
Dendrobium moniliforme
Dendrobium monophyllum
Dendrobium musciferum
Dendrobium rhodopterygium var.
    semialba
Dendrobium virgineum
Dendrochilum glumaceum
Dracula chestertonii
Epicattleya Dora Tinschert 'Spring-
    dale' HCC/AOS
Epidendrum phoeniceum
Gongora horichiana
Iwanagaara Appleblossom 'Fantastic'
Laelia lundii
Lycaste aromatica
Lycaste bradeorum
Lycaste brevispatha
Lycaste ciliata
Lycaste cochleata
Lycaste cruenta
Lycaste lanipes
Lycaste locusta
Masdevallia Confetti

Masdevallia agaster
Masdevallia cyclotega
Maxillaria ochroleuca
Maxillaria seymouriana
Meiracyllium trinasutum
Miltoniopsis Bert Field
Miltoniopsis Hajime Ono
Odontoglossum pendulum
Odontoglossum pulchellum
Oeniella polystachys
Oncidium concolor
Oncidium maculatum
Oncidium microchilum
Phalaenopsis Desert Red 'Ruby'
Phalaenopsis Orchid World 'Bonnie
    Vasquez' AM/AOS
Phalaenopsis Orchid World 'Roman
    Holiday' AM/AOS

Phalaenopsis Sweet Memory 'Amy
    Dawn' AM/AOS
Phalaenopsis amboinensis
Phalaenopsis gigantea
Phalaenopsis lueddemanniana
Phalaenopsis modesta
Phragmipedium Wilcox AM/AOS
Pleurothallis cocornaensis
Pleurothallis ramulosa
Polystachya Darling Star
Potinara Twentyfour Carat 'Lea'
    AM/AOS
Rhyncholaelia glauca
Stelis pusilla
Trichopilia suavis
Vanda dearei
Vanda denisoniana

Spring to Summer Blooming

Aerangis appendiculata
Aerangis brachycarpa
Aerangis confusa
Aerangis kirkii
Aerangis kotschyana
Aerangis mooreana
Aerangis somalensis
Angraecum compactum
Angraecum didieri
Angraecum magdalenae
Ansellia africana
Brassia verrucosa
Bulbophyllum odoratissimum
Cattleya Peckhaviensis
Cattleya forbesii
Cattleya granulosa
Cattleya mossiae
Cattleya schilleriana
Cattleya warneri
Coelogyne lawrenceana

Cycnoches chlorochilon
Cycnoches warscewiczii
Cymbidium eburneum
Dendrobium chrysotoxum
Dendrobium macrophyllum
Dendrobium parishii
Dendrobium williamsonii
Doritaenopsis Phoenix Fire 'Cardinal'
Encyclia adenocaula
Encyclia phoenicea
Encyclia tampensis
Epidendrum difforme
Epidendrum inversum
Laelia purpurata var. werckhauseri
Lycaste Aquila 'Détente' FCC/AOS
Masdevallia glandulosa
Masdevallia laucheana
Masdevallia mejiana
Miltoniopsis Celle 'Wasserfall'
    AM/AOS

Miltoniopsis Hamburg 'Red Velvet'
Oncidium crispum
Oncidium ornithorhynchum 'Lilac
   Blossom'
Oncidium tigrinum
Paphiopedilum Armeni White
Phalaenopsis Wes Addison 'Blood
   Brother'
Phalaenopsis hieroglyphica
Polystachya bella
Rangaeris amaniensis
Rhyncholaelia digbyana
Rhynchostylis coelestis

Rhynchostylis retusa
Schoenorchis fragrans
Sedirea japonica
Spathoglottis deplanche
Thunia marshalliana
Trichocentrum Nathakhun
Trichocentrum tigrinum
Trichoglottis philippinensis 'Pololei'
Vanda coerulescens
Vanda cristata
Zygopetalum Artur Elle 'Tanzanite'
   AM/AOS

Summer Blooming

Aerangis mystacidii
Aerides crassifolia
Aerides falcata
Aerides fieldingii
Angraecum eichlerianum
Bothriochilus bellus
Brassolaeliocattleya Arthur Bossin
   'Rapture'
Bulbophyllum comosum
Bulbophyllum suavissimum
Catasetum candida
Catasetum collare
Catasetum expansum
Catasetum roseum
Cattleya labiata
Cattleya warscewiczii
Cymbidium cyperifolium
Dendrobium antennatum
Dendrobium bellatulum
Doritaenopsis Garnet Elf 'Mary'
Epidendrum parkinsonianum
Jumellea densifoliata
Masdevallia triangularis

Maxillaria rufescens
Maxillaria sanderiana
Maxillaria tenuifolia
Oncidium cucullatum
Peristeria elata
Phalaenopsis Dotty Woodson
   'Claudette' HCC/AOS
Schoenorchis gemmata
Sobennikoffia humbertiana
Stanhopea candida
Stanhopea cirrhata
Stanhopea costaricensis
Stanhopea ecornuta
Stanhopea grandiflora
Stanhopea jenischiana
Stanhopea oculata
Stanhopea pulla
Stanhopea reichenbachiana
Stanhopea saccata
Stanhopea tigrina
Stanhopea tricornis .
Stanhopea wardii
Trichoglottis wenzellii

Summer to Fall Blooming

Aerides falcata var. houlletiana
Aerides odorata
Aerides quinquevulnera
Angraecum birrinense
Brassavola cucullata
Brassia longissima 'Pumpkin Patch'
Bulbophyllum hamatipes
Bulbophyllum lobbii
Bulbophyllum rothschildianum
Catasetum Orchidglade 'Davie
   Ranches' AM/AOS
Catasetum fimbriatum
Catasetum integerrimum
Catasetum warscewiczii
Cattleya aclandiae
Cattleya dowiana
Cattleya guttata
Cattleya maxima 'Mountainside'
Cirrhopetalum graveolens
Cirrhopetalum ornatissimum

Coelogyne fimbriata
Cycnoches
Cycnoches ventricosum
Cymbidium Golden Elf 'Sundust'
   HCC/AOS
Gongora galeata
Gongora leucochila
Haraella odorata
Laelia tenebrosa
Lycaste deppei
Lycaste powellii
Masdevallia attenuata
Miltonia regnellii
Miltonia schroederiana
Miltonia spectabilis
Miltonia spectabilis var. moreliana
Miltoniopsis roezlii
Neofinetia falcata
Trichocentrum albococcineum
Zygopetalum crinitum

Fall Blooming

Aerangis articulata
Angraecum Lemforde White Beauty
Angraecum Longiscott 'Lea'
Brassavola flagellaris
Catasetum maculatum
Cattleya Chocolate Drop 'Kodama'
   AM/AOS
Cymbidium sinensis
Cymbidium tracyanum
Dendrobium wardianum
Dendrochilum cobbianum

Dendrochilum magnum
Gongora quinquenervis
Laelia anceps
Laelia perrinii
Laelia rubescens
Oncidium longipes
Sigmatostalix radicans 'HMO's Petite
   Prince'
Vanda roeblingiana
Zygopetalum intermedium

Fall to Winter Blooming

Aerides lawrenceae
Aerides lawrenceae var. sanderiana
Angraecum eburneum
Catasetum discolor

Cycnoches loddigesii
Diaphananthe pulchella
Epilaelia Beverly Shea
Eurychone rothschildianum

Lycaste leucantha
Rhynchostylis gigantea
Rhynchostylis gigantea Sagarik Strain
Rhynchostylis gigantea var. alba
Rhynchostylis illustre

Tuberolabium kotoense
Vanda tesselata
Vanda tricolor
Vanda tricolor var. suavis
Zygopetalum mackayi

Winter Blooming

Acampe papillosa
Acineta superba
Amesiella philippinense
Angraecum Veitchii
Angraecum aporoides
Angraecum bosseri
Angraecum sesquipedale
Brassavola Little Stars
Brassolaeliocattleya Formosan Gold
Brassolaeliocattleya Goldenzelle
   'Lemon Chiffon' AM/AOS
Brassolaeliocattleya Haw Yuan
   Beauty 'Orchis'
Brassolaeliocattleya Hawaiian
   Avalanche
Brassolaeliocattleya Pamela Hether-
   ington 'Coronation' FCC/AOS
Brassolaeliocattleya Ports of Paradise
   'Emerald Isle' HCC/AOS

Bulbophyllum ambrosia
Bulbophyllum cocoinum
Cattleya quadicolor
Cymbidium mastersii
Dendrobium Gai Quest
Dendrobium Jesmond Fancy
Dendrobium Light River
Dendrobium Sea Mary 'Snow King'
Dendrobium delicatum 'Brechts'
Dendrobium heterocarpum
Dendrobium speciosum
Dendrobium unicum
Diaphananthe pellucida
Jumellea sagittata
Laeliocattleya Angel Love
Lycaste Imschootiana
Lycaste Walnut Valley 'Black's
   Glow'
Trichopilia fragrans

Winter to Spring Blooming

Angraecum leonis
Cochleanthes amazonica
Coelogyne cristata
Dendrobium draconis
Dendrobium Jesmond Gem
Dendrobium Spring Bride
Dendrobium Spring Doll
Dendrobium jenkinsii
Dendrobium lawesii
Dendrobium primulinum var. gigan-
   teum
Laelia albida
Leptotes bicolor

Leptotes unicolor
Masdevallia livingstoneana
Maxillaria picta
Oncidium cheirophorum
Paphiopedilum emersonii
Paphiopedilum kolopakingii
Paphiopedilum malipoense
Phalaenopsis fasciata
Phalaenopsis mannii
Phalaenopsis schilleriana
Polystachya fallax
Zygoneria
Zygopetalum maxillare

Variable Blooming

These orchids can flower different times of the year and sometimes bloom multiple times in one year.

Aerangis biloba
Aeranthes Grandiose
Angraecum boisserianum
Angraecum distichum
Angranthes Grandalena
Anguloa clowesii
Ascofinetia Cherry Blossom
  'Delicado'
Beallara Marfitch 'Howard's Dream'
  AM/AOS
Brassavola Yaki 'Black's Best'
Brassavola cordata
Brassavola martiana
Brassavola nodosa
Brassavola tuberculata
Brassidium Dragon Flight 'Fluff'
Brassocattleya Binosa 'Kirk'
  AM/AOS
Brassocattleya Mt. Hood
Brassolaelia Memoria Bernice Foster
Brassolaelia Sarah Black
Brassolaelia Yellow Bird
Brassolaeliocattleya George King
  'Serendipity' AM/AOS
Brassolaeliocattleya Momilani
  Rainbow
Brassolaeliocattleya Rio's Green
  Magic
Bulbophyllum beccarii
Bulbophyllum echinolabium
Bulbophyllum laxiflorum
Bulbophyllum phalaenopsis
Cadetia chionantha
Cadetia taylori
Catasetum gnomus
Cattleya Brabantiae
Cattleya Fascelis
Cattleya harrisoniana

Cattleya intermedia
Cattleya intermedia 'Carlos'
Cattleya walkeriana var. alba
Cochleanthes Moliere
Cochleanthes discolor
Coelogyne Intermedia
Coelogyne pandurata
Coelogyne zurowetzii
Coryanthes bruckmuelleri
Coryanthes leucocorys
Cymbidium ensifolium
Cymbidium kanran
Darwinara Charm 'Blue Star'
Dendrobium Chrystaline
Dendrobium Comet King 'Akatsuki'
Dendrobium Sweet Song 'Memory'
Dendrobium anosmum
Dendrobium aureum
Dendrobium nobile
Dendrobium nobile var. virginale
Dendrobium pugioniforme
Dendrochilum arachnites
Encyclia citrina
Encyclia cordigera
Encyclia fragrans
Encyclia lancifolia
Encyclia polybulbon
Encyclia radiata
Encyclia trulla
Epidendrum ciliare
Epidendrum falcatum
Epidendrum nocturnum
Eria gigantea 'Waterfield'
Eria hyacinthoides
Gongora grossa
Gongora pleiochroma
Gongora unicolor
Jumellea confusa

Laelia pumila var. *coerulea*
Laeliocattleya Angel Love
Laeliocattleya Hausermann's Sultan
Laeliocattleya Jungle Festival
Laeliocattleya Mari's Song 'CTM 217'
    HCC/AOS
Laeliocattleya Mini Purple
Laeliocattleya Nora's Melody
Laeliocattleya Whitiniae
Lycaste Alan Salzman
Lycaste Lucianii
Milpasia Leslie Garay
Milpasia Milt's Choice 'Helen of
    Troy'
Miltoniopsis phalaenopsis
Miltoniopsis santanaei
Neostylis Lou Sneary
Neostylis Lou Sneary 'Blue Moon'
Neostylis Lou Sneary 'Pinky'
    AM/AOS
Odontioda Vesta 'Charm'
Odontobrassia Fangtastic Bob
    Henley
Odontocidium Tiger Crow 'Golden
    Girl' HCC/AOS
Oncidium Gold Dust
Oncidium Issaku Nagata 'Volcano
    Queen' HCC/AOS
Oncidium Sharry Baby
Oncidium Sharry Baby 'Misaki'
Oncidium Tsiku Marguerite
Oncidium Twinkle 'Fragrance
    Fantasy'
Oncidium Twinkle 'Red Fantasy'
Otaara Haw Yuan Bay 'She Shu'
Paphiopedilum Joyce Hasagawa
Paphiopedilum Lynleigh Koopowitz
Paphiopedilum delenatii

Phalaenopsis Caribbean Sunset
    'Sweet Fragrance'
Phalaenopsis Ember 'Blumen Insel'
    AM/AOS
Phalaenopsis Kilby Cassviola 'Sweet
    Fragrance'
Phalaenopsis Mary Lillian Taylor
    'Desert Orange' AM/AOS
Phalaenopsis Mini Mark 'Holm'
Phalaenopsis Perfection Is 'Chen'
    FCC/AOS
Phalaenopsis Samba
Phalaenopsis Valentinii
Phalaenopsis bellina
Phalaenopsis violacea
Polystachya campyloglossa
Polystachya cultriformis
Polystachya mazumbaiensis
Polystachya pubescens
Potinara Burana Beauty 'Burana'
    HCC/AOS
Potinara Free Spirit 'Lea' AM/AOS
Ronnyara Manuel Ugarte 'H & R'
Sophrolaeliocattleya Haw Yuan Star
    'Pink Lady'
Stanhopea embreei
Tuberolabium odoratissium
Vanda Pat Delight
Vascostylis Crownfox Red Gem
Vascostylis Tham Yuen Hae 'Blue
    Queen' HCC/RSPC, JC/AOS,
    HCC/AOS
Woodwardara Adelaide
Zygocolax
Zygopetalum
Zygopetalum BG White 'Stonehurst'
    HCC/AOS, AM/AOS
Zygopetalum Redvale 'Fire Kiss'

Appendix G

Sources for Fragrant Orchids

Most orchid sellers have at least some fragrant offerings, but some suppliers consciously breed for fragrance or search out crosses that have fragrance potential. These are the sources in the following list. Some of them offer mail order while others also sell at their greenhouse. The list is by no means complete, but will get you started. You can also check out the Web. The American Orchid Society (AOS) has an excellent Web site that lets you search for suppliers by geographic location. The society publishes *Orchids*, a magazine with additional sources. In fact, joining AOS, is highly recommended for the many resources it provides.

The Web addresses have not been given in this list, since they are subject to frequent change and can be found easily with any search engine.

Andy's Orchids
734 Oceanview Avenue
Encinitas, California 92024
Phone: (888) 514-2639
Fax: (888) 632-8991
E-mail: info@AndysOrchids.com

This company grows over 3000 species. Its Web site has a very effective search engine that allows you to search for fragrant orchids. The last time I used it, I came up with a list of more than 100 fragrant orchids for sale. The Web site is also very informative and gives helpful cultural information.

Big Leaf Orchids
4932 Longwood Court
Irving, Texas 75038
Phone: (972) 659-1406
Fax: (972) 659-1438
E-mail: phal@bigleaforchids.com

Peter Lin, owner of this small, backyard company, loves phalaenopsis and has a special affection for the fragrant ones. Check out his Web site for some quality clones and crosses. The site hosts a highly informative phalaenopsis forum.

Cal Orchids

1251 Orchid Drive
Santa Barbara, California 93111
Phone: (805) 967-1312
Fax: (805) 967-6882
E-mail: info@calorchid.com

Owners Lauris and James Rose have been in the orchid business since 1970. They offer some choice fragrant species and hybrids including select neofinetias and their hybrids, as well as a good selection of angraecoids, miscellaneous cymbidiums, and brassavolas. Web-only catalog.

Countryside Orchids

P.O. Box 958
Corrales, New Mexico 87048
Phone: (505) 263-6888
Fax: (505) 792-9807
E-mail: billschn@aol.com

This company offers an absolutely mind-boggling range of mostly species, but some hybrids and mericlones. The on-line catalog is highly informative and indicates which orchids are fragrant. An amazing resource!

Gold Country Orchids

390 Big Ben Road
Lincoln California 95648
Phone: (916) 645-8600
Fax: (916) 645-7076
E-mail: gcorchids@aol.com

Owner Alan Koch is one of the few orchid breeders putting a great deal of effort into producing compact and miniature cattleyas that have fragrance. Among the conspicuous species in his work are *Cattleya aclandiae, C. walkeriana,* and *C. luteola,* along with other sweetly scented species such as *Rhyncholaelia digbyana* and *Brassavola nodosa.* His Web site offers on-line ordering.

Ha'iku Maui Orchids

2612 Pololei Place
Ha'iku, Hawaii 96708
Phone: (808) 573-1130
Fax: (808) 572-7015
E-mail: haikumaui.orchids@
verizon.net

Norman Mizuno, the president of this company, is from New York where he grew prize-winning orchids under lights. He specializes in orchids and selected forms that are easy to grow. His printed and on-line catalogs include a broad selection of fragrant orchids which are prominently marked as such. The company makes special efforts to grow their plants under lower light conditions so they will adapt well to growers in mainland United States.

Hoosier Orchid Company

8440 West 82nd Street
Indianapolis, Indiana 46278
Phone: (888) 291-6269
Fax: (317) 291-8949
E-mail:
orchids@hoosierorchid.com

The company offers a broad selection of species, including an extraordinary number of angraecoids, most of which are fragrant. It also includes other genera noted for fragrant species, such as *Zygopetalum* and *Stanhopea*.

I. N. Komoda Orchids
P.O. Box 576
Makawao, Hawaii 96768
Phone/Fax: 808-572-0756
E-mail: orchidhi@maui.net

Owner Ivan Komoda specializes in and breeds primarily miltoniopsis but offers some masdevallis and other species. He is developing pink forms with waterfall patterns and has often used *Miltoniopsis santanaei* (profiled in this book) to give warmth tolerance and fragrance. He has no catalog, but offers specials in *Orchids* magazine ads and has a Web site.

J & L Orchids
20 Sherwood Road
Easton, Connecticut 06612
Phone: (203) 261-3772
Fax: (203) 261-8730
E-mail: jlorchid@snet.net

A miniature orchid lover's paradise. The highly knowledgeable owners, Cordelia Head, Marguerite Webb, and Lucinda Winn, know their orchids and are very familiar with which ones are fragrant. Their print and on-line catalogs also indicate if the plants are fragrant.

Lauray of Salisbury
432 Undermountain Road
Route 41
Salisbury, Connecticut 06068
Phone: (860) 435-2263
E-mail: jbecker@mohawk.net

Owner Judy Becker is an AOS judge, so knows her orchids and is specifically knowledgeable about some of the fragrant ones. She assisted me greatly with this book, and she and I are working to offer more fragrant orchids to our customers. Her company offers a broad range of orchid species and hybrids, as well as some nice orchid companions like begonias, gesneriads, and succulents.

Norman's Orchids
11039 Monte Vista Avenue
Montclair, California 91763
Phone: (909) 627-9515
Fax: (909) 627-3889
E-mail: support@orchids.com

This company has the most useful and easy-to-navigate site for purchasing orchids on-line that I have experienced. You can search by various requirements—light needs, flower color, plant size, fragrance—to come up with a list of orchids that fit your needs. Then you can store the names of these orchids in your wish list until you're ready to purchase plants. The company has a series of fragrant phalaenopsis as well as a very broad selection of other fragrant species, hybrids, and clones. On-line catalog only.

Porter's Orchids

10868 Royston Road
Grand Ledge, Michigan 48837
Phone: (888) 622-7643
Fax: (517) 622-4188

This company specializes in orchids that are easy to grow and bloom and are well suited to home culture. It offers a broad range of hybrids and species, a good number of which are fragrant and marked as such on the on-line catalog.

Phoenix Orchids

2807 West Villa Rita Drive
Phoenix, AZ 85053
Phone: (602) 938-3741
E-mail: phxorchids@msn.com

Owner Eric Goo breeds phalaenopsis. His various crosses and meristems focus on the reds and yellows, a good number of which are fragrant. Web catalog only.

Glossary

axil the angle between the upper side of a leaf and the stem from which it
grows

column the central part of the orchid flower that contains both the male
(stamen) and female (pistil) parts

cultivar a cultivated variety

deciduous dropping the leaves; not evergreen

dormant a state of inactive growth

epiphyte, epiphytic a plant that grows on another and gets its nutrients
from air and moisture

grex a group of hybrid plants with the same parents

hybrid a cross between two plants, generally of two different species or
genera

intergeneric involving two or more genera

keiki a plantlet. The Hawaiian word for *baby.*

lip the lowermost petal of an orchid flower, usually different from the other
two petals in shape, color, and size

inflorescence the arrangement of flowers on an axis

mericlone a plant derived from tissue culture that is genetically identical to
its parents

meristem undifferentiated tissue that can develop into specialized tissues
or new organs

monopodial a type of growth habit in which the plant continues to grow
vertically from its tip. Examples: phalaenopsis, vandas

pendulous hanging downward

proboscis a long, hollow tube attached to the head of an animal and used
for taking in food and drink

pseudobulb the thickened (bulb-like) stem of many orchid plants

raceme an unbranded flower stem in which the flowers are borne on short stalks and usually open from the bottom of the stem to the top

rhizome a root-bearing stem found on sympodial orchids

sepal one of three outermost parts of an orchid flower

sheath a modified leaf that encloses developing flower bulbs

spike an unbranched flower stem with many stalkless flowers

spur a tubular or sac-like extension of an orchid flower, generally containing nectar

subterete somewhat cylindrical

sympodial a type of growth habit in which a new shoot arises from the rhizome of the previous growth. Examples: cattleyas, oncidiums

terete cylindrical

terminal at the end of a stem

terrestrial a plant that grows in or on the ground

throat the opening in the lip of an orchid flower

umbel a flat-topped flower stem in which all the flower stalks originate from the same point on the stem

vandaceous having a growth habit like that of the genus *Vanda* in which the leaves grow in two rows

Bibliography

Ackerman, Diane. 1990. *A Natural History of the Senses.* New York: Random House.

Atwood, John T. 1994. Maxillarias. *American Orchid Society Bulletin* 63 (4): 372–383.

Averyanov, Leonid, Phillip Cribb, Phan Ke Loc, and Nguyen Tien Hiep. 2003. *Slipper Orchids of Vietnam.* Portland, Oregon: Timber Press.

Baker, Margaret L., and Charles O. Baker. 1991. *Orchid Species Culture: Pescatorea, Phaius, Pholidota, Phragmipedium, Pleione.* Portland, Oregon: Timber Press.

Bechtel, Helmut, Phillip Cribb, and Edmund Launert. 1986. *The Manual of Cultivated Orchid Species.* Revised edition. Cambridge, Massachusetts: MIT Press.

Bock, Rob. 2004. Stunning Stanhopeas. *The Orchid Review* 112 (1255): 43–46.

Cash, Catherine. 1991. *The Slipper Orchids.* Portland, Oregon: Timber Press.

Chadwick, A. A. 1997. A new look at *Cattleya dowiana. Orchids* (July): 678–685.

Christenson, Eric A. 2001. *Phalaenopsis: A Monograph.* Portland, Oregon: Timber Press.

Dressler, Robert L., and Glenn E. Pollard. 1976. *The Genus Encyclia in Mexico.* Mexico: Asociacion Mexicana de Orquideologia, A.C.

Dunmire, John R., and editors of Sunset Books. *Orchids.* Menlo Park, California: Sunset Books.

Fitch, Charles Marden. 2000. Fragrant orchids. *Orchids* 69 (4): 322–333.

Fitch, Charles Marden. 2002. *Growing Orchids Under Lights.* Delray Beach, Florida: American Orchid Society.

Fitch, Charles Marden. 2004a. *The Best of Orchids for Indoors.* Brooklyn Botanic Garden All-Region Guides. Brooklyn, New York: Brooklyn Botanic Garden.

Fitch, Charles Marden. 2004b. *The Gardener's Guide to Growing Orchids.* Brooklyn Botanic Garden All-Region Guides. Brooklyn, New York: Brooklyn Botanic Garden.

Fowlie, J. A. 1970. *The Genus Lycaste: Its Speciation, Distribution, Literature, and Cultivation—A Monographic Revision.* Pomona, California: Day Printing Corporation.

Frowine, Steven A. 2005. *Orchids for Dummies.* Hoboken, New Jersey: Wiley Publishing.

Genders, Roy. 1977. *Scented Flora of the World.* London: Robert Hale.

Goldner, William R., David H. McMahon, and Jochen Heydel. 1997. Orchid aromas: analysis to essence. *Orchids* (March): 265–271.

Gordon, Bob. 1985. *Culture of the Phalaenopsis Orchid.* Rialto, California: Laid Back Publications.

Grove, David L. 1995. *Vandas and Ascocendas and Their Combination with Other Genera.* Portland, Oregon: Timber Press.

Hamilton, Robert M. 1977. *When Does It Flower?* British Columbia, Canada: Robert M. Hamilton

Hansen, Eric. 2000. *Orchid Fever.* New York: Vantage Books.

Hennessy, Esmé F. 1989. *The Slipper Orchids.* Randburg, South Africa: Acorn Books.

Herz, R. S., C. McCall, and L. Cahill. 1999. Hemispheric lateralization in the processing of odor pleasantness versus odor names. *Chemical Senses* 24: 691–695.

Hetherington, Ernest. 1985. *Cattleya* hybrids and hybridizers, yellow cattleyas 1. *American Orchid Society Bulletin* 54 (2): 149–159.

Hetherington, Ernest. 1986a. *Brassavola digbyana*—the unsung patriarch. *American Orchid Society Bulletin* 55 (3): 122–131.

Hetherington, Ernest. 1986b. *Cattleya* hybrids and hybridizers, prospects for the future. *American Orchid Society Bulletin* 55 (5): 452–461.

Hillerman, Fred E. 1992. *A Culture Manual for Angraecoid Orchid Growers.* Grass Valley, California: Fred Hillerman.

Hillerman, Fred E., and Arthur W. Holst. 1986. *An Introduction to Cultivated Angraecoid Orchids of Madagascar.* Portland, Oregon: Timber Press.

Howard Hughes Medical Institute. 1995. *Seeing, Hearing, and Smelling the World.* Chevy Chase, Maryland. Http://www.hhmi.org.senses.

Kaiser, Roman. 1993. *The Scent of Orchids: Olfactory and Chemical Investigations.* F. Hoffmann: Basel, Switzerland.

Kamemoto, Haruyuki, and Rapee Sagaraik. 1975. *Beautiful Thai Orchid Species.* Bangkok, Thailand: The Orchid Society of Thailand.

Kranz, Frederick H., and Jacqueline L. Kranz. 1971. *Gardening Indoors Under Lights: A Complete Guide.* New York: The Viking Press.

Lai, T. C. 1985. *Noble Fragrance: Chinese Flowers and Trees.* 2nd edition. Kowloon, Hong Kong: Swindon Book Company.

Lavarack, Bill, Wayne Harris, and Geoff Stocker. 2000. *Dendrobium and Its Relatives.* Portland, Oregon: Timber Press.

Martin, Tovah. 1991. *The Essence of Paradise: Fragrant Plants for Indoor Gardens.* Boston: Little, Brown and Company.

Miranda, Francisco E. 1990. Brazilian laelias—Part 1, section *Cattleyodes. American Orchid Society Bulletin* 59 (3): 234–245.

Motes, Martin R. 1997. *Vandas: Their Botany, History, and Culture.* Portland, Oregon: Timber Press.

Nakamura, Shoji, Katsuhiko Tokuda, and Akihiko Omao. 1990. Japanese Prize Fragrance Competition. *American Orchid Society Bulletin* 59 (10): 1031–1036.

Nash, Ned. 1996. Flavor of the month, *Cymbidium ensifolium. Orchids* (September): 972–974.

Northern, Rebecca Tyson. 1970. *Home Orchid Growing.* 3rd edition. New York: Van Nostrand Reinhold.

Rentoul, J. N. 1982. *Growing Orchids: Book Three, Vandas, Dendrobiums, and Others.* Portland, Oregon: Timber Press.

Ritterhausen, Brian, and Wilma Ritterhausen. 2002. *The Practical Encyclopedia of Orchids.* London: Lorenz Books.

Rose, James. 1994. *Neofinetia falcata* hybrids. *American Orchid Society Bulletin* 63 (4): 384–391.

Schelpe, Sybella, and Joyce Stewart. 1990. *Dendrobiums: An Introduction to the Species in Cultivation.* Gillingham, Dorset: Orchid Sundries.

Scully, Robert M., Jr. 1975. *Catasetum* Orchidglade—A colorful new hybrid. *American Orchid Society Bulletin* 44 (8): 715–719.

Sense of Smell Institute. 1996. *Living Well with Your Sense of Smell.* Rev. ed. New York: Sense of Smell Institute.

Sessler, Gloria Jean. 1978. *Orchids and How To Grow Them.* Englewood Cliffs, New Jersey: Prentice-Hall.

Sheehan, Tom, and Marion Sheehan. 1994. *An Illustrated Survey of Orchid Genera.* Portland, Oregon: Timber Press.

Siegerist, Emly S. 2001. *Bulbophyllums and Their Allies: A Grower's Guide.* Portland, Oregon: Timber Press.

Soule, Lee C. 1990. Fragrance in orchids. *American Orchid Society Bulletin* 59 (7): 700–703.

Szyren, Jan. 2003. Without high phosphorous: A new fertilizer proves itself with orchids. *Orchids* (June): 454–459.

Teo, Chris K. H. 1985. *Native Orchids of Peninsular Malaysia.* Singapore: Times Book International.

Van der Pijl, and Calaway H. Dodson. 1969. *Orchid Flowers: Their Pollination and Evolution*. Delray Beach, Florida: American Orchid Society.

Watson, James B., ed. 2002. *Orchid Pests and Diseases*. Delray Beach, Florida: American Orchid Society.

White, Judy. 1994. The nose knows. *American Orchid Society Bulletin* 63(2): 118–124.

White, Judy. 1996. *Taylor's Guide to Orchids*. Boston: Houghton Mifflin.

Williams, Louis O., and Paul H. Allen. 1980. *Orchids of Panama: Monographs in Systematic Botany*. St. Louis: Missouri Botanical Garden.

Withner, Carl L. 1988. *The Cattleyas and Their Relatives*. Portland, Oregon: Timber Press.

Plant Name Index

Boldface numbers indicate photo pages. For more listings of fragrant orchid species and hybrids, see appendices A through G.